Bullying

Effective strategies for long-term improvement

David Thompson, Tiny Arora and Sonia Sharp

London and New York

First published 2002
by RoutledgeFalmer
11 New Fetter Lane, London EC4P 4EE

Simultaneously published in the USA and Canada
by RoutledgeFalmer
29 West 35th Street, New York, NY 10001

RoutledgeFalmer is an imprint of the Taylor & Francis Group

© 2002 David Thompson, Tiny Arora and Sonia Sharp

Typeset in Sabon by
Keystroke, Jacaranda Lodge, Wolverhampton
Printed and bound in Great Britain by
TJ International Ltd, Padstow, Cornwall

British Library Cataloguing in Publication Data
A catalogue record for this book is available
from the British Library

Library of Congress Cataloging in Publication Data
A catalog record for this book has been requested

ISBN 0–415–23092–6 (hbk)
ISBN 0–415–23093–4 (pbk)

Contents

Tables

Preface: series introduction

School staff face many challenges today. Recently they have had to respond to a plethora of curriculum and assessment reforms, Literacy and Numeracy Strategies, Government-led moves towards performance indicators, regular OFSTED inspections, and a general push towards accountability and raising achievement levels of pupils. But there are other, possibly more enduring, concerns that also affect the day-to-day functioning of schools.

I get insight into these concerns in the course of one of my professional responsibilities – supervising teachers who are undertaking research for dissertations, as part of MA-level courses. When choosing a topic I encourage them to reflect on their own professional concerns and ways in which they can shed light on them. The range of topics is rich and varied and in recent years has included underachievement of particular groups in school, student motivation and attitudes, bullying, effective approaches to inclusion in classrooms, and pupils' emotional and social difficulties. Some issues are made particularly pressing because of recent events in their own or neighbouring schools, and are high on agendas of current educational and political discussion, as well as at staff meetings.

However, too often the information teachers and others need on these topics is not available in a form that they find helpful or accessible. Sometimes the topic is addressed in a way that is too academic and removed from the practical concerns of everyday school life. But there is a converse problem that seems to have become more obvious recently – a tendency to oversimplify and trivialise what is likely to be a complex issue, and offer packaged solutions instead of a full analysis.

This book series – School Concerns – has been set up to bridge the gap between these two types of approach. It was designed to address contemporary issues, usually related to behaviour in schools, that are cause for concern. The aim of each book in the series is to summarise and evaluate relevant research evidence and theory, and to seek to provide insights, conclusions and suggestions of value to readers, and to relate research findings and theory to classroom concerns. The series is designed to be helpful but to avoid a 'cook-book' approach, to do justice to the complexity of a topic while avoiding dense argument and jargon. This is a difficult balance to achieve, but each author has been chosen because it was felt that not only was he or she a leading authority on a particular topic, but he or she would also be able to make the topic accessible to a wide audience.

The publishers were keen to start the series because, as far as they knew, there has not been an attempt to cover these kinds of issues in a unified and accessible fashion. The series covers both primary and secondary sectors.

Each author has been asked to think carefully about the potential readers of the book. We have asked each author to include, as an integral part of the book, a case study of a class or school and to use this to illustrate and exemplify key ideas and conclusions. The books should be of interest to all in schools, to tutors and students on Initial Teacher Training and Professional Development Courses, as well as to researchers and lecturers, LEA and government staff. The books will also be of interest to a wider and more general audience – for example, parents. Some issues are of obvious international interest and authors have been encouraged, where appropriate, to draw out conclusions of relevance overseas.

This is a timely and exciting series, and I expect the books to provide a significant contribution to educational debate.

Introduction to this book

This is a timely book. There has been a lot of concern about bullying in schools, which has been inflamed by high-profile cases of children who have suffered, with sometimes tragic consequences. Past research has shown that bullying in schools has been underestimated and not always taken seriously enough. This has put staff in schools in a difficult position, with understandable cries that more could have been done to help. But this raises questions about what staff *can* do about bullying, and this book by David Thompson, Tiny Arora and Sonia Sharp is an important contribution.

There are dangers in oversimplifying the causes of bullying and the ways of dealing with it; there are also dangers in overcomplicating the issue or conducting research that has limited relevance in practice. I feel that this book succeeds in avoiding both extremes. It is a careful coverage of the main issues involved in understanding what bullying is and the ways of intervening effectively. It is particularly timely in addressing long-term issues connected to bullying – in terms of the origins of bullying and also the need for a long-term perspective on interventions.

The authors have been working on this topic for a number of years, and in this book they put together their findings and conclusions. There is a thorough review of what we know from research, but also sound advice on what to do. It is grounded in the school experience of bullying, with particular cases being highlighted. This is a book that manages the difficult trick of being relevant to all concerned with this issue: to teachers, policy-makers, school managers, parents, and also researchers and academics.

Professor Peter Blatchford
Institute of Education, University of London

Introduction: an overview

Bullying has been a part of school culture for a long time and, apart from one or two far-sighted academics (Lowenstein 1978; Olweus 1978), there was virtually no research carried out into the topic before 1980. Almost all researchers were deterred by the difficulties of definition and the way in which bullying seemed to be a part of social life in schools. In addition, the impossibility of experimental manipulation, or even simulation, of the bullying process by researchers made the difficulties of conducting research greater. The organisational sensitivities of schools and colleges meant school staffs did not want to admit to the issue for fear of their public image. There has been an explosion of research during the last ten years, but some schools are still justifiably anxious about tackling bullying in too open a fashion. They fear that such anti-bullying action by staff may be interpreted as indicating that there was a severe problem in the first place. Anxiety over disclosure influences the victims as well as the schools, and many young people and their parents keep their problems to themselves. However, in 1991 the Department of Education in the UK gave a research grant to Professor Peter Smith in Sheffield, to fund an intervention study in the city (Smith and Sharp 1994; Sharp and Smith 1994). This built on the collections of writing put together previously by various authors and editors to record what schools were doing to combat bullying (Besag 1989; Roland and Munthe 1989; Tattum and Lane 1989). In 1994, the Department for Education in the UK published 'Don't suffer in silence', a set of in-service training materials for schools, arising from the Sheffield research. Since then, most schools in the country have felt much more supported by educational administrators and advisers in the Local Education Authorities, consultants of various sorts and researchers, so that they can begin to tackle bullying with some hope of success. Researchers have built up a general picture of many of the issues of concern around bullying, and these will be detailed and expanded on in the following sections.

This book aims to provide an insight into the current issues associated with bullying in schools, and in particular how bullying begins, and how the extent of bullying in schools can be reliably assessed and changes in the extent of bullying measured. It goes on to discuss how anti-bullying initiatives can be set up and how these initiatives can be designed to maintain their effectiveness over the years. Questions are posed which teachers, parents and child carers may ask themselves about children's bullying, and we go on to discuss research findings accumulated over the past ten years which are beginning to tell us something about the nature of bullying. In doing so, we gradually build up our understanding of the social settings in which bullying occurs and how these settings can discourage or encourage the spread of bullying. The book also highlights the emerging questions for future research and practice. The complexity of the bullying process is emphasised throughout, but care is also taken to highlight which actions can be taken to reduce bullying substantially, not only in the short term, but also over longer time periods. The book is intended to be useful to school managers, teachers, parents, and child carers, and also to researchers and students.

Bullying appears to be related to how children learn to deal with aggression from their fellows as they grow up from the middle childhood years onwards, as it is very definitely a process which happens among peer groups, with little contact from adults. Many of the children concerned – both the 'bystanders', who are not directly involved, and the victims, who unfortunately are involved – have very useful insights into bullying. Most children learn to use aggression appropriately and how to deal with situations where others are threatening them with violence or being verbally abusive. Some find learning these skills much more difficult. Chapters 1 and 2 look at these areas and the ways in which the search for dominance and affiliation play a part in the development of patterns of bullying. Some discussion is also included of factors which protect children against victimisation. Gender differences exist in the ways in which children bully others, as they do in many other developmental progressions, and these are included as far as the available research evidence permits.

Lack of obvious methods of defining bullying, and of assessing its incidence, was one of the major reasons why there was so little research into bullying until comparatively recently. Chapter 3 looks at ways of assessing bullying. Researchers evolved methods to do this in the period 1975–1985, using two different styles of questionnaire. Both concentrated on 'asking the children', as opposed to asking parents or teachers. One approached the problem of definition by letting the children define what they called bullying (Arora 1994). The other defined bullying in adult terms, then simplified the definition and asked children if this had happened to them (Olweus 1978).

Arora (op. cit.) listed a number of negative actions between children in school, enquired if the children had experienced them, and then asked children: 'If this happened to you, would you call it bullying?' This method gave the additional advantage that it identified particular activities which most of the children (and their teachers, too, incidentally) saw as constituting bullying, and so identified the core activities involved in bullying as most commonly defined. This method also gave a way of finding out what proportion of the group of children concerned saw this activity as being 'bullying'. This is highly relevant when considering activities such as name-calling, which is often quoted by adults as a core part of bullying, whenever it occurs. Children, however, recognise that name-calling often also occurs outside bullying situations, and only a minority of them include name-calling as a core element of bullying. What seems to be important is the nature of the name-calling and its context, not whether it occurs at all. The resulting questionnaire – the Life in School checklist (Arora 1994) – has been used in a number of types of school context across the country, and because it bases the definition of bullying on relatively simple and direct actions, and does not use the word 'bullying' anywhere in its text or titles, has been readily translated into other languages. Translating the word 'bullying' into other languages can often be difficult, as some languages (for example, French and Greek) do not have a single word equivalent to the British and Scandinavian concept of bullying which carries the same social meaning (Fabre-Cornelli, Emin and Pain 1999). Whether or not the language holds a directly equivalent concept to the English 'bullying', however, the pattern of systematic aggressive activity constituting bullying is readily recognised by native speakers of languages other than English. Wherever aggression among school children is a concern, the anti-bullying research gives a useful body of knowledge about how this particular form of social aggression develops and provides a guide to intervention.

The other, earlier approach adopted by Scandinavian researchers to the problem of definition and assessment was that pioneered by Olweus in Norway in the 1970s and thoroughly described by him in the context of a review of anti-bullying research in Norway (Olweus 1999). This was to construct as good a definition of bullying as possible with the knowledge then available, translate it into as simple language as possible so that children could both understand and read it, and include that definition in a questionnaire for children designed to assess incidence and discover other features of the bullying. The resulting questionnaire has been used by researchers in the UK, Ireland and Scandinavia to explore bullying activities in schools. The fact that the methods used to assess the incidence have been relatively standard when either of these two questionnaires has been used has been very useful, in enabling different researchers to assess the incidence of bullying across different situations with a degree of consistency and with a body of knowledge about incidence in other situations using the same instrument. One study has even used the two questionnaires together (Ahmad 1997) to assess how the reported incidences changed from one method to the other. The second method of assessment of incidence and associated factors, of including the word 'bullying' and its definition in specifically designed questionnaires, has also been used by researchers investigating other aspects of bullying (for example, Branwhite 1994). Both these ways of defining and assessing bullying, and other extensions to these proposed by researchers and practitioners, are discussed in Chapter 3. This chapter also looks at how the reported incidences of bullying can change if differing definitions are used.

To date the most institutionally authoritative definition in the UK, in the sense that it was the first definition constructed by a judge in the UK for legal purposes to do with court cases for damages, is:

> Bullying is long-standing violence, physical or psychological, conducted by an individual or group and directed against an individual who is not able to defend himself in the actual situation, with a conscious desire to hurt, threaten or frighten that individual or put him under stress.
>
> (Heald 1994).

This definition is, in fact, based on definitions used by researchers and extended to include features of intention. The 'intent to hurt' is difficult to insist on in research situations because of the difficulties in being sure how far the child who bullies does intend to hurt as opposed to express their own domination over others, but 'intent to hurt' makes a good deal of sense for the community at large and is an important element in the criminal code.

Susceptibility to bullying and the social conditions for it to occur

Some of the research to date has been concerned with what we know of the personalities of the bully and the victim. More recently some clues have been emerging as to how early patterns of child-rearing may contribute to children being predisposed towards adopting the role of aggressor, victim or bystander in playground interactions. However, for most children, involvement in the bullying incidents, both as bullies and as victims, is short term and partial, in that the bullying occurs only infrequently. For these children the particular circumstances in school are crucial in determining whether the bullying occurs or not, and how long it lasts, rather than their personality attributes. Chapter 1 looks at how bullying emerges as a part of the social life of young children. Chapter 2 explores these issues of the social conditions under which bullying occurs, and Chapter 3 looks at the processes involved in bullying and how frequently they occur, and also considers information from international comparisons.

Bullying as researched outside the United Kingdom

Throughout the study of bullying, researchers have been interested in trying to make international comparisons, both as a source of alternative ways to deal with the phenomenon and as a source of new issues for research. This section will consider how far the experience of overseas educators mirrors that of those in the UK. Cultures differ in their response to aggression amongst people in their daily life, and some also ascribe a certain amount of aggression as a normal part of self-expression, for boys and men in particular. The extent of detailed anti-bullying work differs in different countries, but there is enough to make it possible to explore how far bullying is a universal phenomenon and how variable the methods would have to be to influence significantly this aspect of children's behaviour. Researchers have explored these issues in detail in

Scandinavia, the Netherlands, Canada, and Australia (as well as in a number of other European countries) although, interestingly, less so in the USA. There, researchers tend to concentrate on much narrower, individualised aspects of child behaviour and avoid relating the behaviour to issues of school culture or the wider social culture. Smith *et al.* (1999) have collated a number of accounts from different countries in which researchers across the world explore the problems of definition and incidence in their own countries.

Chapter 4 looks at the impact of bullying on the victimised child. One of the areas underlying the interest in bullying is the evident distress of the victims, and the extent to which bullying itself is associated with stress and other psychosomatic and physical health problems is only just beginning to be researched. The fact of the association is established, but the mechanism whereby the psychological stress translates into physical symptoms has yet to be specified. When children suffer social stress they develop psychological mechanisms to deal with the stress and the situations in which they find themselves. Part of the harm resulting from bullying is caused because these coping mechanisms themselves distort the normal patterns of development for the child. For example, they may develop the habit of avoiding making contact with any children whom they do not know already, due to anxiety about possible aggressive contacts from them. Chapter 4 goes on to consider what the possible ways might be of minimising long-term disruption to the child's emerging personality.

Bullying does not happen only in school, however. It continues into the family, the workplace, and closed institutions such as the army and prison establishments. The details of the patterns of behaviour will change slightly across this range of organisations, and the way the bullying roles are constructed by the individuals concerned will vary also. One of the key areas where long-term bullying outside school occurs is in the family, and particularly in the phenomenon of wife-battering and child abuse. At present, these are defined under the criminal code in terms of direct physical aggression and 'mental cruelty', with the creeping assumption that the men involved are pathologically disturbed or psychologically inadequate. However, the model of adult bullying can become further developed to one where the bully gains systematic psychological advantage out of the bullying behaviour. These patterns of using aggression as a normal part of relationships between men and women do not, however, appear out of thin air – they are learnt from the patterns of social relationships between boys and girls which are developed in adolescence and which are demonstrated during school years. Duncan (1999) gives a detailed picture of the part which can be played by aggression and violence in emerging relationships between boys and girls in school, which underline the seriousness of systematic aggression in schools for later patterns of living. These are additional theoretical explanations to that of mental disturbance or inadequacy in the adult bully or victim. They are derived from the study of childhood bullying, and relate to the systematic social and emotional advantages which may result from maintaining a very dominant position in the family group, for no other reason than the systematic use of aggression and violence. A similar alternative and additional use of the model of bullying behaviour may also fit violent relationships between the sexes – as another explanation of sexual harassment. This may begin as an attempt to use aggression inappropriately in developing relations between girls and boys in school – a form of sexual bullying. Existing theories of sexual aggression are developing at present, with the general recognition of the role that power relationships have in the motivation of sexual assaults and rape. In the same way, the motivation of bullies does not seem to be dependent on the specific material gained from the bullying behaviour, but in the expressions of power and re-affirmation of the identity of the bully as dominant.

Effective intervention

Chapter 5 returns to the research on bullying in school, particularly looking at the research into what makes some interventions effective and others less so. This is based on two major studies on the effectiveness of a number of interventions. Some implications of this work stress the importance of clearly stated anti-bullying policies, which are widely understood by everyone in school. To increase understanding and ownership, these policies and procedures should have been worked out through consultation with all interested parties, including children, and should influence the operation of the pastoral care system in school. The implications of the research also emphasise the significance of training and induction policies for teaching and non-teaching staff, and the effective operation of whole-school behaviour policies and anti-racism policies. Specific materials included in the curriculum which stress social support for others have been shown in the anti-bullying research to be a potentially significant agent for positive change, especially in primary schools.

However, even when a school has successfully established an effective anti-bullying policy, and has evidence that it is working, the little long-term follow-up research we have seems to indicate that many schools find it difficult to maintain the efforts as a normal part of their work. The situation can easily deteriorate again to its original level, or even to a worse level that it was at before. A minority of schools do manage to maintain the system, however, and for them the level of bullying continues to go down. Chapter 5 looks at the factors which enable schools to keep up the good work. Discussion of these factors includes areas often considered more under the management of schools than associated with anti-bullying work. These are areas such as the role of the project leader in the school, the school as a learning organisation, and the use of support from outside agencies and consultancies.

High levels of bullying amongst pupils may form one source of general but diffuse stress on the majority of staff and pupils, even if they are not directly involved, and through them such levels of bullying may reduce the effective implementation of school procedures and may impair school organisation. In this way, bullying in school, and the resulting stresses between pupils, may be seen as one example of a range of general features which produce stress on school organisations, such as generally disruptive pupil behaviour, rapid staff turnover and unrealistic external expectations of schools. Dealing with stresses related to bullying then relates to ways in which the school might protect itself against the whole range of such stressors, at both a pupil and a staff level, through management-led processes such as those involving clarification of values, expectations of behaviour inside school, and keeping effective communications between staff, pupils and parents.

One of the issues as yet relatively unresearched is the nature of support for schools from LEA staff and private consultancies, who can help the staff manage the policies most effectively. At present we have the experiences of some researchers, who have become involved, in their roles as collectors of information from the schools, in helping them assess levels of bullying, and the experiences of a small number of staff in LEAs where a systematic attempt has been made to support schools. These experiences are also explained and discussed in Chapter 5.

Differences between schools

Another of the intriguing findings of previous research is that some schools appear to be much better than others at instituting and maintaining effective anti-bullying procedures as part of effective behaviour policies. Why? What are the differences, and how can schools be encouraged to adopt the most efficient procedures? One interesting corollary of this is the general tensions between 'top-down' management systems in anti-bullying work and the feelings and reactions of those working directly with the children. These are similar to those tensions often felt in other parts of the educational system from similar sources. When the effective procedures can be described, will it be sufficient for school managers and the Office for Standards in Education (OFSTED) to say, 'Do this' for the procedures to be effective, or will the whole process need to be worked through as a social priority inside the school? Again, there are some clues in existing research, and these are explored further in Chapter 5.

Managing whole-school change

Much has been learned from the efforts of schools about how to implement anti-bullying policies and procedures in schools and how to co-ordinate these with other concerns and policies, such as the behaviour policy and staff development policy. The various officers of the LEA and agencies of central government such as OFSTED also have their different roles to play in supporting schools to set up and maintain anti-bullying projects. In Chapter 6, the details of implementing these whole-school programmes are worked through, with the implications for the development of support services.

Specific responses to bullying behaviour

Many schools have gathered experience in implementing specific programmes to reduce bullying in the classroom and playground as a part of their more general, whole-school initiatives. Chapter 7 describes a range of specific approaches which can be used, both those involving group work approaches and those addressing individual needs of the pupil being bullied and the pupil showing the bullying behaviour. Group work methods include such procedures as establishing peer counselling support systems in schools, using quality circle techniques with the pupils to discuss problems related to bullying and what the class group can do in response, and adapting teaching materials to emphasise generally co-operative behaviour amongst the pupils. Individual methods include the Method of Shared Concern and the No Blame Approach, when working with the pupils who bully others, and social skill training, including assertiveness training, when working with the pupils who are bullied.

Future research issues

Chapter 8 considers the research issues that are emerging from the various sets of studies. The first major issue is the theoretical one of the validity of considering the bullying process itself as a useful focus of research, rather than the more detailed aspects of behaviour already identified in theories of child development. These more detailed aspects may include such developmental changes as the process of social dominance, the role of aggression in the social development of children, and the impact of stressors of various kinds on psycho-social development. Much may be learned about bullying behaviour by researching further into the role of the peer group in encouraging pro-social behaviour, and the ways that all these patterns of behaviour can be influenced by the behaviour policies and practices in the public school system. A number of researchers into bullying have concentrated on bystander behaviour as a point of access. At least one researcher in the field (Arora 1996b) holds some belief in the view that bullying is too general a concept to continue to focus research and intervention upon, due to the variable definitions of bullying which may be used by researchers in any given project. If different research projects use different definitions of bullying, then any differences in rates of bullying reported from the projects are very hard to interpret. The differences may be due to the different school situations investigated, or to the different definitions used, or to a combination of both. Many researchers, however, still continue to focus on the general concept of bullying, because they believe the pattern of behaviour identified as bullying is a sufficiently stable one to be easily recognised in schools and elsewhere. They would claim that bullying is also sufficiently well recognised in most communities to be a cause for concern, which leads to social support for the research from teachers, parents and the wider community. This general concern for recognising and limiting bullying also makes people interested in the results of the research.

Since 1990, more and more has been learnt of how complex the bullying process can be and of how bullying changes in different situations. Future research will explore the details of bullying in different situations. At present, we know that bullying amongst older pupils seems to be different in some ways to bullying among younger pupils, with fewer pupils involved but the bullying relationships more stable. Girls seem to bully in a different way to boys, with less dependence on physical threat and more involvement of social exclusion. Successful interventions to reduce bullying can be based on different theories, with, for example, some interventions stressing common co-operative values amongst all children and others specifically focusing on interrupting the relationship between the pupil who bullies and the pupil who becomes the victim.

The rest of Chapter 8 examines the various specific research questions which have emerged so far from the literature and from developing practice. At the generic level, these include such issues as the overlap (if any) between the concepts of bullying and racial harassment, and of bullying and sexual harassment. If there are similarities between the ways in which these various social processes occur, how true will it be that an effective programme to reduce one may also have an impact on the frequency of the other forms of harassment?

At the more specific level, one of the general findings to emerge from the research on the characteristics of victims is that some children are more vulnerable to bullying than others, usually having poorer social skills in interacting with their peers and poorer skills in asserting themselves. Some of these characteristics are found in children with special needs, whether or not they are educated in mainstream schools. Future research projects will discover how schools can operate so as to identify and support such children, to ensure that the extra difficulties they face in learning are not made worse by being the victims of bullying processes.

Collaboration between staff undertaking research

One of the intriguing facets of the previous and current research into the bullying process and ways to overcome it is the interaction between academic researchers and practitioner researchers. Sometimes, on large projects, both types have been in the same research teams, but frequently they have been listening to each other and, in turn, picking up the issues, methodologies and procedures described by each other. Perhaps certain issues of the overall research programme are more accessible to researchers from one institutional membership than to those of the other. On the other hand, bullying, due to its complexity and dependence on the specific social context, is an example of a phenomenon that is inaccessible to researchers unless they do communicate effectively across the academic–practitioner divide and across academic disciplines. Certainly it is not a topic which can be approached directly in any kind of laboratory setting, and the essentially covert nature of almost all bullying means that the staff of the school has to be centrally involved in the research activity for it to have contact with the community in which the bullying occurs. Chapter 8 considers carefully the possible ways of managing research into bullying, involving the strengths of both practitioners and academic researchers, so that the projects are productive.

After all the research, however, the network of organisations that constitutes the education system of today has to absorb and implement the findings of the research. The needs of users of research have to be considered at the time when the research projects are designed. How is this to be achieved? It can be claimed that the educational establishment has already gone further than it usually does to recognise the outcomes of research – for example, the DfEE recognised the social significance of the early research work on bullying at the end of the 1980s, funded the first major intervention project in the UK, and made the results of the project and in-service training materials available free to every school in the land which asked for it. Later on, the OFSTED inspectors were meant to include questions about a school's anti-bullying policy in their standard list of questions for schools and, in anticipation of this, many schools suddenly developed a keen interest in developing anti-bullying policies. With all this recognition, might we expect the incidence of bullying to have been reduced? There seems little evidence so far.

Longitudinal research studies, studying the same schools over a period of two to four years using the same instruments, are few and far between. Some individual schools that have been systematically monitoring their own progress in reducing bullying using questionnaire surveys may have some very interesting data in their files. The few longitudinal studies we do have, however, suggest that the expectation of a consistent reduction in bullying over time in most schools with anti-bullying policies is based on very false premises (Eslea and Smith 1998; Thompson 1995; Roland and Munthe 1997).

The evidence seems to indicate that many schools, perhaps the majority, who at one time have successfully reduced bullying through anti-bullying programmes, will find it difficult to maintain the effect unless they specifically continue the activities in the anti-bullying project at the same level of intensity. The incidence of bullying can easily creep up to its original level again in a matter of two or three years. Maybe the parallel should be with the teaching of reading – would many teachers assume a two-year programme to be sufficient to teach reading and that, after the initial push, they could relax and turn to teaching maths instead? If bullying is to be successfully reduced in UK schools, the anti-bullying policies and procedures need to be extended from the usual current levels to include long-term, quantitative surveys of the effectiveness of the policies in each school and, if the levels of bullying show a rise from one year to the next, to include reviews of procedures. In turn, this will need co-operation between school staff, local authority support staff with training in quantitative evaluation, and possibly professional researchers from higher education. It seems unreasonable to expect school staff by themselves to be able to set up such long-term research projects, and certainly experience to date suggests a little external consultative help at the project design stage, or help at the data analysis stage, can make a considerable difference. After the projects are set up, however, school staff would be able to continue to run them, if the school system included giving such priority to anti-bullying work.

In Chapter 9 the main conclusions from the book are drawn together and the route to reducing bullying consistently in the UK is sketched out. Bullying and resisting bullying are shown to be closely associated with the social learning of pupils at many stages in their school life. Managing schools and school systems so as to support pupils in developing their skills in handling aggression from their classmates needs co-ordination of roles and policies right across the educational world. Everyone, including the pupils themselves, is involved.

Some questions to think about

- Should efforts to reduce bullying be left to schools?
- What support for anti-bullying work could, and should, be given by central government?
- Should knowledge and skills to enable pupils to resist bullying

continued

be included in the national curriculum, at the cost of time spent on traditional academic subjects?

- Is bullying a sufficiently important topic for measures of bullying to be included in the group of benchmark indices considered when schools are inspected?
- Should the issue of bullying in schools become an equality issue, due to the possibility that it is in schools that aggression towards girls becomes an accepted part of gender relationships for some boys?

Part I

Understanding bullying

Chapter I

The emergence of bullying

The uncertainties for teachers and parents

When teachers and parents are working with and caring for young children, controlling their behaviour is a central concern. From the youngest ages, some children disturb their carers by appearing to want to behave aggressively whenever they feel like it, or when their desires are thwarted. Frequently this tendency leaks into their relationships with other children. Everyone's instinct is to intervene quickly and stop this expression of aggression. Some carers would go further and remove toys such as toy guns and knives. They think such toys encourage aggressive games and initiation of the aggression the children see almost every day on the media. Others reject this approach and claim that children have to learn how to react appropriately to aggression from other children and to be assertive with others in the correct context. Consequently, they would claim that a blanket ban on the expression of aggression is unnecessary, very difficult to achieve, and may possibly be harmful by giving the message that when children want to be aggressive they have to do so outside adults' view.

By the time children reach primary school age they have learnt some of these lessons. These include both the positive ones of expressing and dealing with aggression appropriately and the negative ones of maintaining the freedom to behave aggressively as the mood takes you by keeping aggression out of the way of adults, as teachers and parents have a predictable tendency to interfere and stop you. The general problem does not go away, it just goes underground.

For carers and teachers of young children, therefore, questions needing urgent and flexible answers are: 'When do I stop the expression of aggression quickly and when do I attempt to modify the behaviour to teach the children a better way of asserting themselves without hitting or threatening others?' For the answers to come at the speed that classroom activity requires, the carers have to recognise what is happening and know what to do almost instinctively. Teachers and carers have to be able to distinguish between habitual aggression and one-off incidents. When children repeat behaviour patterns, this tends to indicate that the pattern is being incorporated into the child's habitual way of dealing with different situations, as a part of the emerging personality. When teachers or parents realise this they usually begin to take definite steps to stop the child acting in this way. However, as children's activities become habitual, the behaviour also typically changes in ways that make the expression of the feeling easier but maintain the significance of the behaviour. This occurs through cutting down the length and intensity of the activity, substituting verbal aggression for actual physical aggression, and incorporating the aggressive behaviour into other more neutral behaviours to hide it from the adult attention. Such modified and covert aggression can be just as damaging to the victim as the initial raw expression of anger, but is often seen by the carers as being of less significance.

Some carers may respond according to the extent of the obvious hurt of the child who is the target of the aggression. The greater the hurt, the quicker the aggressive behaviour is stopped. They also recognise the norms, established by the school headteacher and expected by parents, governing teacher behaviour. These tend to be blanket bans on aggression, which may have the unintended consequence that children never learn better ways of dealing with their own or other people's aggressive impulses.

The emergence of bullying

The behaviours associated with bullying can be seen from a very early age. However, these can be termed bullying only when children have reached a certain level of awareness and understanding. Many of the ways of reducing bullying depend on the children being aware that what they are doing is called bullying, and that it is not an acceptable way to behave because of its consequences for the victims and the other children in the group. Some researchers suggest that bullying can be conceptualised as 'a special form of aggression, which is social in its nature' (Bjørkqvist, Ekman and Lagerspetz 1982: 23). This means that the relationship between bullying and aggression needs to be examined. Bullying is mostly a proactive form of aggressive behaviour, with concepts such as intention, motivation, punishment and reward all relevant factors in this complex process. It not only hurts the victim, but also restricts the development and life-chances of the bully by providing a simple and often effective way of attaining a limited social status in a dependent group of classmates (Arsenio and Lemerise 2001). The study of dominance provides us with further clues about the motivation and rewards which are associated with bullying. Finally, research into how children learn prosocial and moral behaviour is a pertinent one for considering how to avoid creating situations in which bullying is rife. This is exemplified by the research of Warden and Christie (1997) and Christie and Warden (1997).

The early emergence of bullying behaviours

Imagine two young babies sitting next to each other, a girl and a boy. The boy has a rattle and is shaking it vigorously, with obvious delight. The girl watches him intently for a few seconds, then snatches the rattle from her companion, who starts to whimper. The perpetrator smiles, waves the rattle and hits the unfortunate victim, who by now is crying piteously. An adult intervenes and says to the girl: 'you bully!'. It will not surprise the audience to see that she looks unconcerned and continues to shriek with pleasure.

Not many people would agree that bullying had taken place on this occasion – yet someone forcefully took a possession, hurt another child, showed pleasure at the child's reaction and unconcern when told off. In older children, all of these behaviours would be typical of a bullying situation. People would argue though that in this case, the baby did not know that she should not take the rattle, did not realise that her actions were the cause of distress, had no intention to hurt and was not aware of the other's feelings. So the emergence of bullying is related to the way children learn to express themselves and learn to empathise with each other as members of the same social group. The above behaviour could be called bullying only if there is an intention to hurt or upset, if the perpetrator has an awareness of cause and effect, an understanding of social norms and rules and an ability to empathise with others' feelings. In short, a certain level of development of thought, as well as social and emotional development, is required to bully. These developments happen quite early in life for most children. By the time they have reached the age of 4 (i.e. the age at which they normally enter school in the UK), they show some of the behaviours commonly associated with bullying, as well as the awareness specified above. Hatch (1987) found that children aged 4 to 6 achieved social power in three main ways: self-promotion, put-downs and dominating others through ordering, threats and physical intimidation. It is not certain to what extent the children understood any hurt they caused, but at this age they were aware of the rules of 'no aggression', and the effects of put-downs, threats and violence. The possible lack of awareness of hurt caused to others could be a vital factor in the understanding of bullying and in interventions to reduce bullying (Pikas 1989; Sullivan 2000).

Bullying and its relationship to aggression

Bullying is clearly a form of aggression. The study of aggression, which has a much longer history than that of bullying, gives us insights into the bullying process. Some caution is necessary, though; Tedeschi (1984) notes how, near the end of the most bloody century in the history of mankind, there had been little progress in the study of aggression.

Temperamental predispositions towards aggressive behaviour

Whilst there is significant evidence to support genetic predisposition towards features such as emotionality, sensation-seeking and impulsivity, there is little evidence to suggest any genetic tendencies or temperamental factors that make a child more likely to be aggressive or violent (Turner 1994). Studies looking for genetic and hormonal influences on aggression and violence indicate that the complex interactions between genetic factors, such as impulsivity and emotionality, and environmental factors, such as parenting style, go on to give a personality basis for the expression of aggression. Torgerson (1995) describes a series of longitudinal studies of children in Finland carried out by Lea Pulkinnen, the first following the children through from age 8 to 20 years. The following two studies concentrated on pre-school children. She concluded that all children have the potential for antisocial and prosocial behaviour. Environmental factors such as parenting style are strong influencers on the eventual outcomes for the child, with the child's own temperament contributing to different types of social interaction difficulties. Turner highlights four key environmental influencers that affect aggressive behaviour: parental attitudes; parental discipline; role models and television violence. The implications of these studies are that for all children and young people we must do our utmost to ensure positive environmental experiences, and most especially for those children with a predisposition towards impulsivity and sensation-seeking. So, all in all, the evidence for aggressive behaviour weighs more heavily towards nurture rather than nature.

Early aggression in schools

One question that is relevant here is whether children who are aggressive in the beginning of their school career have also been aggressive in their pre-school years, and whether children who act aggressively early in life continue to do so at older ages. If we can learn the age at which aggressive patterns of behaviour become stabilised we can provide clues to the timing of preventive work. Loeber and Stouthamer-Loeber (1998) suggest that there has been little research about when and how aggression begins in schools. However, there is evidence of continuity from one Canadian study (Haapasalo and Tremblay 1994), which found that a substantial proportion of boys (8.3 per cent) fought habitually both in the earliest year of their schooling as well as at ages 10, 11 and 12. A further proportion of boys (9.15 per cent) developed aggressive behaviour after their first year in school and continued to be fighters when they were in the 10–12 age range. Similarly, Eron *et al.* (1987) carried out a 22-year longitudinal study of 8-year-old boys in the USA, who had been identified by their peers as aggressive. They found that aggressive behaviour at age 8 was a significant predictor of aggression at later points in their lives. In adulthood, a high proportion had delinquent records and were aggressive towards their wives and children. Longitudinal data analysed by Farrington (1991) in the UK take this even further by showing how men who were known bullies at the age of 8 tend to have children who become bullies. For none of the above studies, however, is it known whether these children were already aggressive before they came to school. These research findings to date support the idea that if boys show aggressive behaviour early in their school career, they are likely to continue to do this later on during their school career and even afterwards. Bowers *et al.* (1994), in a small-scale study, found that children who persistently bully often come from families who used aggressive methods to manage difficult situations.

Reactive and proactive aggression

Roland's (1998) analysis of the relationship between aggression and bullying is a useful one, as it concerns itself with the two main theoretical frameworks developed to explain aggression. Dodge (1991) summarises these as reactive and proactive aggression. Roland points out that it is of great importance, for ethical, theoretical and practical reasons, whether we understand bullying as being proactive (that is, spontaneous or unprovoked, a 'natural' expression of the child's emerging personality) or reactive aggression (that is, aggression in response to something else happening). Each type of aggression has a different set of associated factors, with regard to motivation, reward and feelings engendered on the part of those who bully, as well as indicating a different set of social conditions which permit bullying to happen.

The theoretical view we take also influences the extent to which we see bullying as learned behaviour, which may be susceptible to change, or based in 'aggressive instincts', which will be more difficult to change because they are a part of the emerging emotional make-up of the young personality. Aggression as a reactive behaviour was first described by Freud (1920), who believed that aggression was the result of frustration. Dollard *et al.* (1939), from the background of behavioural theories, developed this concept into the frustration-aggression theory. They proposed that frustration experienced by an individual would continue to build up noxious aggressive energy, which must be released in the form of aggressive behaviour. Such a theory conceptualises aggression as reactive – i.e., it only happens when the individual experiences a feeling of anger against the target or against a substitute, caused by something the target person has done. Aggressive behaviour is then directed towards these targets. It does not assume that the aggressor must have a motive for the aggression, other than to express the feelings of anger. Some evidence that this type of aggression might be involved in bullying is noted in Mykletun's (1979) findings (quoted by Roland 1998): secondary school pupils who bullied reported that they were more likely to be 'irritated by stressful circumstances' than pupils who were victims or who were neutral. So it is possible that there is some relationship between negative feelings and bullying, although one cannot be sure whether this relationship is causal. Roland (1998) draws attention to the fact that Heinemann (1973), who was the first to theorise about bullying (calling it 'mobbing'), saw this purely as reactive aggression, whilst Olweus (1978), an early influential author on the subject of bullying, has taken the opposite view, regarding it as a personality-based, proactive type of aggression.

Heinemann (1973) describes how a group of pupils could become increasingly irritated by one pupil, which would disturb the equilibrium within the group. As a result, the group turns suddenly on this pupil. After the attack, the group quickly returns to normal, having restored the balance within the group. The main emotions felt by the mobbing group would be likely to be anger, followed by relief. A similar example would be the teasing and taunting of a child who is particularly irritating to one or more children. It is difficult, though, to think of many instances of bullying which might be considered examples of reactive aggression.

The model of proactive aggression explains a wider range of bullying behaviour. It assumes that there is usually a specific motive. The behaviour does not necessarily result from feelings of anger or hostility but is intended to gain some reward, although the rewards may be primarily emotional ones. Such a type of aggression does not need a precipitating event for it to occur. Rather, it is behaviour which is learnt through imitation, reinforcement and modelling, although it may be prompted originally by temperamental elements of the young child's physiological make-up. It would help the aggressor to achieve his or her objectives (Bandura 1973) – for example, taking money with threats. In this case, the usual objective and motivation are to gain money and the associated feelings of power and control. The behaviour could have been learnt from peers, siblings, parents, or other significant influences on the child, including fictional characters in books, computer software or television programmes.

Olweus (1978), whose empirical base is much more extensive than that of Heinemann (1973), develops the idea that there are certain personality characteristics, often influenced by home experiences, which create a tendency for children to become bullies or victims. Thus, some children have learnt how to use aggression proactively in order to dominate others or to gain material rewards from them. Their main emotions are likely to be excitement, followed by satisfaction at achieving their objectives.

Bullying as impression management, coercion and/or punishment

The issue of motivation in bullying and the rewards gained is an important one. Proactive aggression can have many rewards – for example, in the case of demanding money with threats, the ulterior motives could be obtaining the money, impressing friends, gaining status, satisfaction at seeing the victim suffer, simple amusement, or a combination of any of these. Out of these, impressing friends or gaining status often appears to be an overriding motive (Thompson and Arora 1991).

The study of aggression in a social context can help to clarify these aspects of bullying. It shows how some bullying behaviours differ from others in terms of the motivation of the bully as well as the extent to which a victim could avoid being harmed (Tedeschi 1984). Tedeschi concentrates on the actual events during an aggressive interaction – in particular, threats, coercion and punishment. He sees threats as a communication from one person to another indicating that that person will receive a punishment in the future. The word 'punishment' is used here to mean any type of negative consequence – it does not imply any wrongdoing on the part of the victim. Threats can be either contingent (punishment will happen as a result of a certain behaviour) or non-contingent (the reasons for the punishment are not clear). Threats can also be explicit or implicit. The most obvious contingent use of threats is to compel compliance from a victim. An act of bullying which is compatible with this is the earlier-mentioned 'demanding money with threats', which clearly has a punishment attached to non-compliance. As has been seen, it also has a gain for the bully if compliance is achieved. The threat here is contingent, in that punishment is promised for non-compliance. In other instances of bullying, the threat may be non-contingent – for example, when a child is informed by the bully that she/he will 'get' him/her after school. On many occasions the victim will not know of any reason for this aggression. For the victim, such non-contingent aggression is likely to be highly anxiety provoking, as there is no obvious way to avoid the threatened punishment. The actual motivation behind this type of act could be impression management strategy (Jones and Pittman 1982). A bully may attempt, by using threats, to establish an identity as tough, resistant to intimidation, and as a member of a group or institution with similar aspirations. The primary motivation would not be to compel but rather to use intimidation. Once a threat is communicated, the source's reputation is on the line. If the threat is non-contingent, or if the victim fails to comply with any specific demands, failure to carry through the punishment lowers the credibility of the source. With bullying, the reaction of the victim to the threat alone is often sufficient to maintain or enhance the bully's status. It would appear that many acts of bullying are forms of non-contingent threats that provoke fear reactions from the victim because of the already established reputation of the bully as a potential punisher. The threat to a victim such as 'I'll get you after school tonight' needs never to be carried out but will provoke upset in the victim, often in the presence of an intimidated audience.

Tedeschi (1984) also distinguishes between four types of punishment: noxious stimulation, deprivation of resources, deprivation of expected gains and social punishments. It is the latter type of punishment that seems to be part of many bullying incidents. Such punishments include name-calling; spreading rumours; making allegations about someone's family, sexual practices or racial group; demeaning rituals; exclusion from groups and institutions. The aim of these actions is to demonstrate dominance by humiliating the victim, perhaps in front of an important audience, and to achieve rejection by or from the group. If one considers the differences between threats and punishments, as outlined above, then one would also need to conclude that bullying is not one type of aggressive behaviour. Rather that one can distinguish different actions by whether they include contingent or non-contingent threats (i.e., respectively, demanding money or threats to hurt someone without an apparent reason) or whether these are solely social punishments without the use of threats (i.e., name-calling, ostracism, etc.).

Tedeschi and Felson (1994) stress that aggression is a means to an end, rather than the end in itself, and that persons use harm for a variety of purposes. The main interactional models are those which are based on impression management, coercive power and punishment. Having already seen how punishment is a variable and complex feature of the bullying process, it would seem that many instances of bullying are a combination of coercion and impression management. For example, someone who fights to display power to an adversary or to others around him (or her), or to maintain the credibility of his or her threats, could be said to be engaging in a coercive form of impression management.

Gender differences in bullying and aggression

Despite obvious biological differences between men and women, there have been few behavioural characteristics that have shown significant differences between the genders. The level of aggression is one of these, with men showing consistently more aggression than women do. Most findings suggest that bullying, as a form of proactive aggression, is reported consistently more by boys than by girls, both as victims and as perpetrators. Differences in aggressive behaviour between boys and girls start early. By the age of 2, boys exhibit more physical aggression than girls do (see, for instance, Hyde 1986). Hartup (1974) shows that these differences remain, although there is a drop in levels of aggression generally between 4 and 7 years. Campbell (1996) points to the significance of the two different types of aggression noted by Hartup. She describes the first one as resource disputes, in which the aggression was about the retrieval of an object, territory or privilege. No sex differences were found in this area, with both boys and girls equally intent on maintaining their possessions or privileges. The second form of aggression was characterised by ego-threats and threats to one's self-esteem. It was this particular form, which the reader might identify as proactive aggression, or bullying, which was significantly higher in boys than in girls. Campbell suggests that this finding is consistent with work on the establishment of male dominance hierarchies (Savin-Williams 1977). She speculates that the early aggressive encounters which boys have about resources tend to become less significant from the point of view of keeping the resource, with a victory more important in terms of their self-esteem and relative status in the group. As they get older, gaining resources is equated with gaining control, with associated effects on status and self-esteem. Thus, boys, when they get older, start to use aggression as a means of gaining status, whereas girls do not. For girls, dominance within the group is not as important as the establishment of affiliation and co-operation. Direct conflict is more aversive to them than to boys, for whom the more obvious way to achieve dominance is by physical aggression or threats. Girls are found to feel less self-control and more guilt and anxiety about acts of direct aggression than do boys as early as 8 years of age (Archer and Parker 1994). These gender differences are well established by pre-adolescence, with girls tending to use 'relational aggression' (Crick and Grotpeter

1995), such as spreading rumours, social exclusion and gossiping, more than boys do, whilst they use less direct aggression (Lagerspetz *et al.* 1988). Why this should be so, is not clear. There are several hypotheses available, depending on whether one favours an explanation based on biological determination, one which is based on environmental or evolutionary factors, or the influence of the interactions of all these (Campbell 1996).

All this research points to a complex relationship between bullying and aggression during the periods when bullying emerges as a distinct pattern of behaviour. Showing aggression does not necessarily mean that a bullying pattern will appear later in a child's development, and when bullying is established, the interactions need not be specifically showing physical aggression. The case study in Box 1.1 looks at some of the issues teachers and parents have to consider when dealing with aggression which may be potential bullying in a young child.

Box 1.1 Case study: a new admission to the nursery at Enderton Primary School

Tom is the older of two children. His younger brother was born prematurely when Tom was 2 years old and has needed a lot of care throughout his young life. Tom did not receive as much attention from his mother as he may have needed, but his father, a successful business man, tried to make up for this by involving him in his own activities and hobbies over the weekends. Tom's father wanted him to be a 'real boy' and felt it was all right for Tom to be aggressive as long as people did not get hurt. He himself had a fiery temper and felt that you needed to 'push' people in order to get things done.

Tom's parents separated when Tom was 4 years old. Tom remained with his mother, who found it difficult to set any boundaries for his boisterous and demanding behaviour.

When Tom entered the nursery class at Enderton Primary School soon after, the staff found him boisterous and insensitive to the other children – when he wanted a toy, he would grab it and often hurt or upset other children as a result. Parents of those children complained about him being a bully.

Tom enjoyed the nursery as there were lots of things for him to play with. He particularly liked the large toys and playing outside on the bikes and toy cars. He would often 'hog' the toys and not let anyone else play with them.

- Are the parents right in calling Tom a bully?
- What could have been factors in Tom's present behaviour?
- How could the staff in the nursery help him?
- Which other people would they need to work with?

Conclusions

From the above analysis it becomes clear that bullying can be seen as a number of different forms of proactive aggression, depending on the motivation and intention of the bully. Boys and girls are likely to be aggressive in different ways and for different reasons, and this may also be apparent in the way they are part of the bullying process. It will also be evident that bullying is a special form of aggression which is social in its nature – that is, it takes the form of certain kinds of systematic, aggressive, social interactions (Bjørkqvist *et al.* 1982). The next chapter will explore this, with particular emphasis on how bullying develops in groups.

Some questions to think about

- Should the degree of hurt to the victims of bullying be the main criterion for adults to take action to reduce the bullying?
- Do children who bully others have to be overtly aggressive in their everyday behaviour?
- How true is it to claim that aggressive behaviour is not something included in the genetic inheritance through early childhood temperament, but is almost completely learnt?
- How true is it to claim that aggressive behaviour is usually a result of pressures inside a social group?
- Why do girls develop different kinds of aggressive behaviour from boys of similar ages?

Chapter 2

The social basis of bullying

The individuality of schools

From the earlier chapters it has been seen that, for some children, bullying is clearly a consequence of some of the complexities of growing up, both at primary school level and at secondary level. Hopefully, being involved in bullying at either age may be a temporary stage which children can learn how to deal with, although this is probably more true for children of primary school age. Schools are one of the key places where children may find themselves being bullied, and much research has been done to describe how schools, as organisations, influence the bullying that happens inside their grounds.

The key questions for schools to ask themselves are:

- How can school staff organise schools so as to make it as easy as possible to encourage children to learn to handle aggression appropriately?
- How do different characteristics of friends, acquaintances and other members of the classroom group of children influence how these skills are learnt?
- How far should the school rely on suppressing bullying by improving supervision in playground areas and corridors to control the more obvious incidents of bullying directly?
- Can any schemes be set up so that children can support each other in a systematic way, rather than turn only to the adults for support?

These are some of the questions that arise in helping children deal with bullying. This chapter looks at the research findings of how schools, as organisations, may influence the extent and type of bullying which occurs, and how far the staff can give the students help to develop a pupil culture which minimises bullying.

Schools, and classes within schools, vary in how much bullying takes place, by quite a considerable degree – up to two and a half times between schools of the same catchment area at both primary and secondary level (Smith and Sharp 1994; Whitney and Smith 1993; Olweus 1991). In addition to this large variation between schools with the same degree of social disadvantage, Whitney and Smith found that schools which scored highly on a scale of social disadvantage were also significantly more likely to experience slightly higher levels of bullying than those with less social disadvantage. The same applied to schools where more students reported being alone at playtime. These general slight differences were considerably less than the possible differences between schools with the same degree of social disadvantage. Ethnic mix of the school population and size of school or class did not relate to variations in levels of reported bullying. These findings have been repeated outside the UK. Ziegler and Rosenstein-Manner (1991) in a study of Toronto schools found higher levels of bullying in inner city schools. In a comparison of adult recollections of being bullied in both single- and mixed-sex schools, Dale (1991) found that there were higher levels of reported bullying in single-sex than in co-educational schools. In general, these studies of differences between schools give a consistent picture – the crucial unit is the school itself, rather than its area or social class mix, but these social class factors do make higher levels of bullying slightly more likely.

Dominance and bullying

The first entry into a new school is a crucial one for the development of bullying. Like adults, when children first come together to form a group, they establish their range of roles, from the dominant to the submissive, within a short period of time. Savin-Williams (1980), in his extensive study of a group of boys attending a summer camp, found that within three days most of the dominance hierarchy had been established. Apart from explanations based on dominance behaviour in animals, there is not a great deal of theoretical explanation available on the reasons for this in human beings. One early experience of dominance is through rough-and-tumble play. This is a form of play fighting in which both partners alternate in being the dominant and receiving side. It involves direct physical contact, without the intention of being physically aggressive. Children rarely get really hurt in such encounters and, unlike bullying, it is therefore seen as a positive rather than a negative interaction. Playground observations in primary schools suggest that boys tend to engage in this more often than girls (Humphries and Smith 1987).

Bullying is thought to be connected with this process of achieving dominance. 'Put-downs', observed by Hatch (1987) in the play of children in the Nursery, were seen as reducing the power bases of the others, whilst other strategies (ordering, threats and physical intimidation) confirmed and added to the dominant child's power base. Whilst rough-and-tumble play occurs less often in the secondary school, the search for status and affiliation continues. Reports from children in a secondary school suggest that bully/victim roles are also established very early on, at the time of the new entry into school. Children who normally use aggression or coercion will attempt to establish dominance and 'show off to their mates' by such means (Thompson and Arora 1991). If sufficient support is gained from admiring pupils or from those seeking the protection of the bully's group, this behaviour can quickly become established as a norm for a number of children in the class. Only direct intervention by the teaching staff can undermine support for the bully. A study of six adolescent girls who had not known each other before (Savin-Williams 1976) found that the most frequently observed behaviours were verbal ridicule, giving a verbal command which was obeyed, and ignoring or refusing to comply with another's demand. The victim's role in this is to provide a suitable target for those who wish to achieve status within the group. For children with some social skills, one strategy to avoid being chosen as a victim is to establish a social relationship with the bully – i.e., to become part of a group of admirers, with some protection from being actually bullied oneself. However, this does not necessarily avoid all aggressive encounters. Everhart's (1983) study of groups of adolescent boys with a taste for aggression showed that being subjected to aggressive acts from members of the group was a way of life. Children may only submit to this if they enjoy playful aggression themselves or if they have the alternative and less desirable choice of being bullied without any support group. In the latter circumstances, the victim may have a different role than that of a complete outsider to the group. Such children may function as fringe acquaintances, or in a general role, such as the clown. This involves accepting, to some extent, the social norms of the group. In some groups, the mutual aggression becomes almost a standardised way of interacting and can become a ritual form of behaviour related to group membership.

The group as an arena for bullying

We have already indicated that bullying takes place when there are a number of children who form an aggressive subgroup, led by a child who tries to achieve and maintain dominance and status within the whole group. If we ask children about their perceptions of what occurs in a bullying situation, they often stress that a bully would find it difficult to maintain the bullying behaviour without the support of other pupils. As already noted, they will also say that the bully's main motivation is to 'show off to his (or her) mates' (Arora 1996a). A bully needs a small group of close supporters, both as helpers and immediate mates to impress, but will also profit from having a larger audience to impress, frighten and intimidate. Olweus (1978) therefore warns that the image commonly held of one bully pouncing on a lonely victim, away from the eyes of the rest of the school, is a rare occurrence. There is now considerable evidence to indicate that there are usually many children involved in a bullying incident. For instance, Craig and Pepler (1992) suggest that peers were involved as collaborators or observers in nearly 90 per cent of bullying episodes. La Fontaine notes that 'it was the presence of the group of onlookers and more passive participants that encouraged the bullying' (1991: 19), in some cases recorded by the Bullying Helpline.

The role of bystanders can have a significant effect on the outcome of a bullying situation. Tedeschi and Felson (1994) note that in adult disputes a variety of roles are adopted by the audience, including instigators, peacekeepers, cheerleaders and bouncers, and that these can have a strong effect on the thoughts, feelings and behaviours of the protagonists. When children were asked about their participation or witnessing of a bullying incident, the roles identified were those of victim, bully, reinforcer of the bully, assistant to the bully, defender of the victim and outsider (Salmivalli et al. 1996b). These will be described in more detail later in the chapter.

Adler and Adler investigated the dynamics of pre-adolescent cliques, such as are found in schools, over a period of seven years. Their study provides a fascinating insight into the power relations of young people and how bullying behaviour is often a function of peer group formation and maintenance. The reader is left with an all too clear impression of the nastiness and brutality of these groups.

Adler and Adler define cliques as

> circles of power wherein leaders attain and wield influence over
> their followers by cyclically building them up and cutting them
> down, first drawing them into the elite inner circle and allowing
> them to bask in the glow of popularity and acceptance, and then
> reducing them to positions of dependence and subjugation by
> turning the group against them
>
> (1995: 145).

The leader of the clique and the other members use bullying tactics
to maintain or boost their own position within the group and to
control the behaviour and attitudes of others. The strategies used by
the cliques included:

- recruitment techniques which promote the exclusivity, and
  therefore the desirability, of the clique;
- deliberate wooing of individuals so that they abandoned their
  usual friendship groups, became isolated and therefore more
  dependent on the clique;
- setting one person against another by using overt ridicule and
  derision;
- picking on low-status people outside the group;
- alternate wooing and derision of people within the group;
- urging others to pick on or ridicule others;
- stigmatising a particular individual and rejecting them;
- expelling someone from the clique.

They quote Craig, a 'clique follower':

> Basically the people who are the most popular, their life outside
> in the playground is picking on people who aren't as popular,
> but are in the group. But the people just want to be more popular
> so they stay in the group. They just kind of stick with it, get
> made fun of, take it . . . They come back every day, you do more
> ridicule, more ridicule, more ridicule, and they just keep taking
> it because they want to be more popular and they actually like
> you but you don't like them. That goes on a lot, that's the main
> thing in the group. You make fun of someone, you get more
> popular, because insults is what they like. They like insults.
>
> (ibid.: 154)

The influence of the clique extends beyond the immediate peer group
and has a significant effect on relationships throughout that year

group. In the UK, these cliques would most certainly match with the descriptions of bullying gangs found in classes that report high levels of bullying. However, the fact that there are just as many classes and year groups which report very low levels of bullying (Smith and Sharp 1994) indicates that the destructive behaviour of Adler and Adler's 'cliques' does not have to be the norm. Arora (1996a) demonstrates that even in the same school, different classes and different year groups can have quite different levels of bullying.

Salmivalli (1998) has researched extensively into the group dynamics of bullying behaviour. She has been able to identify six 'participant roles' which pupils consistently take in classes where bullying is occurring. These are bully, assistant, reinforcer, victim, defender and outsider. The types of behaviour assigned to each role are as follows:

- bully: leading and initiating bullying behaviour; actively involved;
- assistant: becoming actively involved at the instigation of others; supporting the bully;
- reinforcer: providing those directly involved in bullying with positive feedback; acting as an audience; laughing at the victim;
- victim: frequent target of bullying behaviour;
- defenders: providing direct or indirect support to the victimised pupil; trying to stop the bullying;
- outsiders: withdrawing from bullying situations.

In her first study, which involved 573 Finnish pupils aged 12 to 13 years, Salmivalli was able to assign participant roles to 87 per cent of the participants. Pupils were assigned to roles through a process of peer nomination and self-evaluation. She found that there were tendencies for boys to be more frequently assigned the roles of bully, reinforcer or assistant, whilst girls would most often act as defender or outsider. Salmivalli also looked at social acceptance and rejection of the pupils. She found that victimised pupils were very isolated within the class group, scoring low on social acceptance and high on social rejection. She found that boy bullies along with female reinforcers, and assistants scored similarly. Girl bullies were more controversial, scoring above average on both social rejection and social acceptance. Defenders, both boys and girls, scored highest on social acceptance, suggesting that they are the most popular children. Table 2.1 shows the distribution of pupils across the different

Table 2.1 The distribution of pupils across the different participant roles in relation to the four status groups: popular, rejected, controversial and average

Status group	Victim %	Bully %	Reinforcer/assistant %	Defender %	Outsider %
Popular	3.6	10.3	39.0	43.0	29.7
Rejected	71.4	51.3	19.5	22.8	20.8
Controversial	3.6	10.3	4.1	3.8	4.0
Average	21.4	28.2	37.4	30.4	45.5

Source: Salmivalli *et al.* (1996b)

participant roles in relation to the four status groups: popular, rejected, controversial and average.

These studies remind us that an interactionist approach to understanding bullying is important. The bullying relationship is a social relationship, and it is influenced by the social dynamics of the immediate peer group, the wider peer group, the systems and procedures within the school, the ethics and the mores of the community. Children who actively help maintain or assist the bullying may underestimate how important their contribution is. Such children tend to be part of a different and larger friendship network than the victim, defenders of the victim and outsiders are. Victims are often children who are not part of any friendship network (Salmivalli *et al.* 1997).

Influence of emerging gender identity

Teachers recognise the crucial effects of the emerging gender identities of adolescents on their social behaviour. In recent years, more and more research has been done into the detailed structure of social relationships in secondary schools and their effects on the students' behaviour to staff and to each other (Duncan 1999). In practice, these relationships of power and attraction between particular individuals change very quickly, although the general principles driving the relationships do not. The students are learning how to manage these relationships as they grow up during adolescence. When examined in detail, there are found to be considerable differences between schools in the development and structure of gender cultures. These differences include the extent of the aggression involved; the ways the changes for particular individuals are driven by processes of physical maturity, age, or the purposive activities of particular students attempting to dominate the patterns of relationships between their schoolmates for their own ends; and the influence of the adult school culture of acceptable and just-tolerated behaviour (Mac An Ghaill 1995). These cultural differences between schools may well relate to the large variations in incidence of bullying between otherwise similar schools found by some researchers into bullying (Smith and Sharp 1994).

Activities based on the active social management of gender relationships and explicitly sexual relationships between students often involve stable power relationships between particular individuals and groups, as well as a controlled level of aggression or threat of aggression. These often amount to bullying with a gender-based or sexual component. One rather worrying aspect of these interactions, when compared with similar interactions in more loosely structured and individually chosen environments, such as workplaces or further education settings, is the suspicion that the social institution of the secondary school is actively encouraging the emergence of more extreme and more long-lasting patterns of gender-based bullying behaviour than would otherwise be the case in an educational system with a looser structure. They may be doing this by compressing large numbers of students of wildly varying ages, relative maturities, academic abilities and physical characteristics into school buildings for seven hours each day, insisting that they devise social mechanisms to structure their relationships with each other. Schooling in its current form is a socially constructed institution, with historical, economic and even architectural factors very influential and probably dominant over educational and developmental ones. It may very well be the case that such institutions have unintended side effects in terms of encouraging development of patterns of social relationships which are not in the best interests of the children concerned. The danger of this, of course, is that the patterns of behaviour towards the opposite sex learnt in schools during these years may well persist into the post-school years. Duncan (1999) gives a very graphic and readable account of the dynamics of the establishment of these relationships.

These findings from a variety of researchers show that bullying maintains itself by a social process of developmental change. Children are learning ways to structure social relationships based on aggression, into adolescence and adulthood, involving a large number of pupils to a greater or lesser degree, be it voluntary or not (Salmivalli et al. 1997). There will also be varying levels of approval or disapproval from adults and from children for this behaviour. It is assumed that some of the children who approve of bullying would be those who act as the bully or who assist and/or reinforce it. Reports from different countries show that there is a substantial minority of pupils who have this positive attitude towards bullying (Menesini *et al.* 1996), with one survey (Whitney and Smith 1993) quoting 20 per cent of their sample. There may be an age factor in this, although this varies between countries. For example, research carried out in Italy showed that older children were more capable of demonstrating empathy to others than younger ones, which was the reverse of findings in England. On the other hand, children who disapproved of bullying would engage in one or more of the other roles, with attempts to intervene, seek help or be a passive witness.

Learning to deal with bullying and aggression

This section discusses two aspects of the bullying situation: the role of the bystanders and the significance of the victim's response. 'Bystanders' refers to those who are not part of the group that actively supports or reinforces the bullying behaviour. It is important to look at this aspect, as there could be many pupils involved in this role. Also, the degree of social pressure that could be exerted by pupils not directly involved in the bullying process (which comprise approximately three-quarters of the school population) cannot be underestimated. Do they intervene readily? To what extent do they seek help for the victims and from whom? The second aspect is the victim's immediate responses to bullying and the possible effects of these on the maintenance of the bullying. What strategies does the victim use to deal with bullying? What effect do these strategies have on the bullies? The above issues are concerned with the immediate process, rather than the long-term effects on the feelings and behaviour of victims and witnesses of bullying. These long-term effects will be discussed in a later chapter.

The extent to which children do or do not approve of bullying should bear a relationship to their desire to intervene or seek help. However, there is no straightforward link between such attitudes and actual behaviours. Menesini *et al.* (1997) found that girls were more empathetic towards victims than boys but that they were not more likely to intervene. Whilst two-thirds of pupils in their sample agreed that pupils themselves should seek to stop others from bullying, Rigby (1996) noted that less than half of pupils surveyed said that they themselves tried to intervene when they saw it happening. Arora (1996a), in a secondary school with an effective anti-bullying policy, found that secondary boys would not readily intervene once the bullying had started, although they would act as a supportive friend to prevent such bullying in the first place. The possibility of direct intervention had occurred to them, but they had not taken such action, preferring, instead, to draw the bullying to the notice of their teacher. Such a strategy may well be the most helpful one in many cases of serious bullying, as it draws the attention of other, authoritative figures to the problem. However, for many of the more minor bullying incidents, some degree of intervention by other pupils would ensure that every incident was dealt with promptly.

Yet, there is evidence that even telling the staff about bullying, coming from both the victim and the bystanders, is not common in schools without effective anti-bullying policies. It is particularly uncommon for victims: Whitney and Smith (1993), in Sheffield, reported that only half of the children would tell their teachers. Similarly, of the children who talked to the Bullying Helpline (most of whom were girls), only half had already spoken to their parents or teachers before they phoned (La Fontaine 1991). In Australian research (Rigby and Slee 1993) only one in three children (aged 8 to 15) thought they would probably tell their teacher. Four out of five children appeared to admire those who intervene, who 'stand up' for children who are bullied. However, one-third of the children did not agree that it was necessarily 'a good thing' to help children who cannot defend themselves, and about 50 per cent of children did not disagree with the proposition that 'kids who get picked on usually deserve it'. It would therefore seem that those children had an ambivalent attitude towards intervention. Pepler et al. (1993) in Toronto, Canada, with a similar age-group, found that 24 per cent of students reported that they did nothing because it was none of their business, whilst only 43 per cent reported that they would usually try to help. Another third reported that they did nothing, although they felt that they should have done something.

So, despite the fact that quite a high number of children express worry about bullying taking place, even to the extent that they fear going to school (Balding et al. 1998), children are reluctant to intervene.

The sole exception to this came in an interview study of 14-year-old boys in a secondary school where the staff had actively implemented an anti-bullying policy over a five-year period. This entire group said they would tell a teacher if they saw bullying taking place, although they would differentiate between which teachers they would tell (Thompson and Arora 1991). This suggests that a consistently implemented whole-school policy does have some impact on pupil behaviour. There are many possible reasons for non-intervention, some of which may be explained by theoretical models derived from research on bystander support for victims. Staub (1970) suggests reasons why bystanders are reluctant to intervene, although they might have felt they should have, on hindsight. Reluctance to intervene starts to happen with children over the age of 9, younger children being less aware of the social pressures of a situation and therefore more likely to intervene if they perceived another child to be in difficulty. There is evidence that the presence of other people actually inhibits the helping response (Latané and Nida 1981), something that is very relevant to school bullying situations. A number of possible mechanisms may be at work. First, the bystanders may well perceive social pressure not to intervene, with inaction the expected pattern of behaviour. Or, they may expect others to intervene rather than they themselves feeling the need to take any responsibility for action. Or they may well genuinely be concerned that their interventions might lead to reprisals by the bully or the bully's supporters. Another reason sometimes quoted is that the witness is afraid that the intervention may make things worse for the victim. Finally, it is just possible that a school's exhortations to its pupils not to be physically aggressive has the desired effect on non-intervening witnesses, who cannot think of alternative ways of intervening rather than through a fight. There are thus a number of possible reasons for non-intervention, ranging from clearly articulated ones to those of which the bystander may not be immediately aware:

- The victim deserves to be bullied.
- It is not my business to intervene.
- I thought someone else would do something.
- I may make things worse for the victim.
- I am afraid of what the bully and his (her) friends might do to me.
- I will not be able to intervene successfully anyway.
- No one else is doing anything about it either.
- I would make a fool of myself if I intervened.

- I do not know how to intervene in a non-aggressive, effective way.

With such a long list of reasons which may prevent direct intervention by bystanders, together with the fact that it is usually only other children rather than adults who witness the bullying, it is not surprising that bullying is highly resistant to simple one-off intervention procedures by teaching staff. It will be clear that any intervention programme needs to take account of all those possible reasons when trying to persuade the bystanders to take some responsibility for intervention if someone is being bullied. Issues to address would be: Who is responsible for intervention? What support and protection is there available from the school structure for those who intervene? What are successful strategies for intervention and how can we teach these to our pupils? In short, development of the general ethos of a school as well as specific anti-bullying policies will be necessary to achieve positive outcomes in this.

Less is known about the effect of the victim's responses on the bully. Olweus (1978) notes that victims tended to be either passive or provocative, the former being the much larger proportion. These personality characteristics were presented though more as indicators of the children's general behaviour than as the way they might behave when being bullied. Salmivalli et al. (1996a) report that victims showed three different types of responses. The first was to be aggressive in return, the second was to act nonchalant, not bothered, and the third was to be helpless. Girls tended to be helpless or nonchalant, while most boys were aggressive or nonchalant. The best strategy to stop bullying was reported to be nonchalance, with helplessness or aggression prolonging the bullying process. Stanley and Arora (1998) found that girls who were socially excluded tended to use different strategies from those who were not. Their main strategies were passive, whilst those not socially excluded tended to use active, assertive methods.

The development of prosocial behaviour

There is a tendency for people who are involved in trying to reduce bullying to think of this only as behaviour to be stopped. However, in the long-term, behaviour can be stopped only if it is replaced by another, incompatible behaviour. Thus, punishment by itself is not going to reduce long-term bullying. Other, non-bullying behaviours must be developed and taught to replace the previous ones. These are called 'prosocial behaviours'. Like all behaviours, they are accompanied by attitudes and feelings; hence, when considering how prosocial behaviour develops, we must take account of all these various aspects. We have already discussed children's attitudes towards bullying, which can be positive as well as negative and which are complex, depending on their own perceptions of the situation and its consequences. This section considers what prosocial behaviours are, what their motivation might be and how these develop in early childhood.

Christie *et al.* (1994) interviewed children in mainstream and special schools, asking them to describe incidents of social behaviour in which another child had been nice or had done something that pleased them. Teachers and parents were asked a similar question. The behaviours that were identified fell into the following categories:

- sharing: sharing possessions;
- helping: helping with homework, or someone who is hurt, upset; being kind;
- inclusion: befriending, making someone welcome, inviting participation, talking to someone;
- loyalty: sticking up for someone, being altruistic;
- other: not being bad, obeying rules, learning from experience.

Christie *et al.* (1994) then also asked which of these behaviours was considered to be the most important. For the children, sharing was the most important, whilst this came last for the teachers. Loyalty and helping were the two rated as most important by both teachers and parents. For all three groups, inclusion tended to be ranked less high than the other behaviours.

Readers will recognise the above as typical of the behaviours which one would wish children (and adults) to display as part of a caring community. It will also be clear that such behaviours are mostly incompatible with bullying. So what is the basis for these prosocial behaviours? Why do some children share their materials quite happily with others, whilst there are others who do not? Why are some children more aware of what others' needs are and provide for them more readily, by helping or sticking up for them? Some answers to this question may be provided through the work of Howard Gardner. Gardner (1993) questions the traditional view of intelligence as too narrow, based on a concept of intelligence that is restricted to logical and linguistic reasoning. He has identified a further seven types of intelligence: spatial, musical, kinaesthetic, environmental, spiritual, intrapersonal and interpersonal. He argues that each person has their own unique pattern of intelligences, showing marked strengths in one or more. It may be that the 'defenders' described by Salmivalli and colleagues (Salmivalli *et al.* 1996b) are those pupils with strongly developed interpersonal intelligence.

Altruistic behaviour, in particular, has been the subject of many debates. Some sociobiologists argue that an individual should be seen as a collection of genes, each of which has survival as its sole aim. In some species, animals that are related, and which therefore have many genes in common, exhibit helpful or altruistic behaviour towards each other. Thus, the 'selfish gene' (Dawkins 1976) ensures its own survival, irrespective of the individual in which it resides. It can be argued that the same applies to human behaviour, i.e. that which we do for others is for the benefit of our own genes. Whether we agree with the sociobiological explanation or not, it is quite possible to see much of the prosocial behaviour of children as of immediate or longer-term benefit to them. For example, if a child shares sweets with another child the motivation could be to maintain or start a friendship; if a child helps another in distress it may be because the experience of seeing that distress also causes feelings of great concern in the helper. By helping the other child, that feeling of concern is reduced, approval of others is obtained, self-esteem is enhanced, guilt is reduced. This perspective tells us about the possible underlying reasons for prosocial actions. However, whilst we may have an innate tendency towards certain behaviours, a great deal is in fact learnt rather than instinctual. Early learning of prosocial behaviour takes place in interactions with parents, other carers, as well as with siblings and early playmates. Some of these are taught directly, such as when a mother tells her child to share an interesting toy with her sister and praises her when she does so. Others may be learnt incidentally – for instance, when a little boy finds out that being friendly towards his playmate encourages participation in his play with cars and thereby makes it all much more creative and exciting than playing by himself. Often, prosocial behaviours are learnt through imitation of others. We all have seen small children going over to cuddle another child when it is in distress. Whilst the basis for such behaviour may be instinctive, the way it is performed is through copying what adults do in similar situations.

Learning of prosocial behaviours takes place only if there are suitable models and if there are consistent rewards for them. For instance, if the adults in the child's life show little prosocial behaviour there will not be an opportunity for copying this and finding out its benefits. Similarly, if there is no appropriate direct teaching of such behaviours, or if the rewards for these are non-existent, then the child will not have learnt or practised these by the time he or she enters school. In those circumstances, staff in school cannot expect children to learn such behaviours purely by chance. They will need to teach them directly as well as explicitly model them through their own behaviour. This can be achieved effectively only in a school that has a clearly described curriculum for social development that emphasises sharing, helping and caring (Warden and Christie 1997). This theme will be taken up again in later chapters.

Vulnerable children in school

One of the worries among parents of shy or introverted children at most ages is how to prevent them from being bullied. Teachers also from time to time find themselves seeing certain children as more likely to be bullied than others. What do we really know of children who are more vulnerable? Are they the unassertive ones, the isolated ones, the ones at the top of the class – the 'swots'? This theme of the background 'character' of the bully and the victim is surveyed and described very effectively by Besag (1989), and continues to be a popular area of speculation.

The most obvious aspect of a victim's personality is his or her appearance, and bullies often refer to this when questioned about why they were picking on one particular child. However, these comments by the bullies are much less reliable than commonly thought, as there are many children who also share some of the characteristics named by the bullies but who are not chosen as victims. Olweus (1993) is fairly clear that, in general, physical characteristics are not the reason why some children are bullied more persistently. However, some physical characteristics may overlap with more psychologically based reasons, such as isolation, lack of communication with other children, lack of knowledge or mechanisms for making friends. When children are asked in interview studies (for example, Thompson and Arora 1991) how they protect themselves from bullying in schools, the single, universal response was: 'You go around with your mates.' From theoretical considerations and survey research, lack of social skills to make friends and maintain good friendship networks is indeed a crucial element in becoming vulnerable to bullying. Some of the other factors shown to be associated with victimisation – for example, lower self-esteem gained from peer group interactions (Sharp 1997) – may well gain that association through the existence of the more central element of poor social skills, particularly poor social skills in communicating with classmates not sharing class membership or specific interests. Where natural group membership links do not exist between children, then they have to learn actively to construct new links available to them in the classroom and the school. They have to learn to do this from the curricula available in school, including the informal behavioural curriculum and the curriculum of the pupil culture.

Self-motivation and self-control

Some research into social competence of children has shown links to parenting style, parental support and discipline of children, and 'locus of control'. Locus of control describes whether children see their activities as originating in their own wishes and activities (an internal locus of control), or whether they feel that activities and desires were imposed by others from outside (external locus of control) (Swick and Hassell 1990; Bowers *et al.* 1994). Specifically concerning bullying, some research (Sharp 1995) has stressed the importance of children learning to guide their activities through a large measure of their own internal control, so that when they do become involved in difficult emotional situations with their peer group they are used to taking action themselves to get themselves out of it. When children have these skills of starting and actively managing their relationships with their classmates, they are more able to find ways of avoiding unwelcome attentions and are less stressed when such tensions occur. Accordingly, parental styles which encourage children always to look to adults to tell them what to do, and when to do it, are not helping them to develop skills in managing their own relationships.

Children with special needs

Another group of children who have been found to be more at risk from bullying are those with mild or moderate special needs. There has been little research into this aspect of bullying, either in a mainstream school context or in special schools, but what there is, is not very comforting. Whitney and Smith (1993) report the results of the incidence survey for children included in the integrated special needs units in the schools in the DfEE intervention programme in Sheffield in 1991–1992. They found that children in the integrated units reported a significantly greater level of victimisation than the other children in the schools did. They also noted that the teachers of these children were much more aware of the bullying experienced by these children than other subject teachers were of the bullying occurring among mainstream children without special needs. This greater teacher awareness is easily understood as being related to smaller class sizes, a particular interest in the individual children's welfare, and possibly to the greater and more systematic assessment procedures involved with educating children with special needs. But how are we to react to the possibility that children with special needs are more likely to be bullied? This is particularly relevant given the current move towards greater inclusion of children with special educational needs. However, there has been no systematic research into levels of bullying in separate special schools to allow comparisons of results. At present, there is no evidence that children with special needs are more likely to be bullied in mainstream schools than in special schools. When such research is done, the particular type of special school will be of great significance, as we cannot assume that the pattern of social interactions between children who have special needs is independent of the particular type of need. It also is very likely that the finding of the great variations in levels of bullying between schools found in research on mainstream schools will be repeated in research on levels of bullying in special schools. The combined effects of differences between schools based on type of special need provided for and based on individual school culture will be very likely to make it completely impossible to make any claims whatever for any 'general' level of bullying for segregated special schools as a group. The only possibility will be for individual schools to make the effort to work out their own levels of bullying, as described in Chapter 3, and to use that to guide their own pastoral development plans.

If the finding of greater vulnerability of children with special needs to bullying is held up in later research, why might this be so? The integrated units in the study were for children with mild and moderate learning difficulties, so the safest assumption would be that there was a certain amount of general developmental delay amongst the children in the units, when compared with their age-mates in school. One possible factor could be the level of social development and social skills of the children with special needs. This might place them at increased risk of not being able to manage their friendships as fluently as other children. The case study in Box 2.1 illustrates some of the complexity of situations arising from these factors for teachers caring for quite typical groups of children. Also, at the time of this research, these schools offered integrated opportunities for learning, rather than inclusive ones. Inclusive settings adapt to meet the needs of the individual child and, in doing so, pay attention to social inclusion within the peer group. Successful inclusive schools draw heavily on the support by peers of pupils with special educational needs as well as recognising how pupils with special educational needs can support peers in return. This high level of peer involvement may reduce the likelihood of increased bullying and is an area worthy of further research. There would probably be other factors operating as well, but what they are best described as would be purely speculative at present. Chapter 7, which looks at specific interventions to minimise bullying, discusses further what might inform a school's responses.

Box 2.1   Case study: a problem in Year 4 at Enderton Primary School

Shaun, Darren and Paul usually play together during breaks. They are confident boys who like to 'have a laugh' and who often engage in 'play fighting' during the breaks. They come from the same housing estate as Stephen. This estate is one of the main feeder areas for the school. The parents of Shaun and Stephen, who are next door neighbours, often quarrel about the noise of loud music and dogs fouling the play areas.

Stephen is a bit of a loner. He is shy and slightly clumsy and does not easily mix with the other children in the class. His main playmates are one or two girls. He sometimes seems to join in with the other three boys, but this is never on a regular basis. His level of work is well below the rest of the class.

Stephen's teacher was aghast when she found out that Shaun had been telling Stephen to bring 50p for him on a number of occasions over the last month. She heard about this only when Stephen's mother came up to the school, saying that Stephen had been taking money from her purse. When his mother had pressed him, he had told her that he had to take it in for his 'friend'. Further questioning of Stephen elicited that he was often called names (Spaz) by Shaun and his friends and that Shaun only allowed him to play football with them if he gave them money.

Stephen's teacher decided that this was not just a case in which one boy had bullied another by demanding money from him. She needed to find out what the role had been of Darren and Paul in this bullying, as she realised that Shaun may have asked for the money not because he needed it, but to show off to his friends. She also had to establish whether those two boys, and possibly others in his class, were supporting the bullying behaviour. There may also have been children in the class who had known about Stephen's problems but who had not told her about it. Did they approve of what Shaun was doing or did it just not occur to them to tell their teacher? She also needed to make sure that Stephen would tell her if something like that happened next time.

- How can the teacher stop these bullying behaviours?
- Would she need to intervene with the small bullying group, with the whole class, or with both?
- What support does she need from other school staff?
- What wider aspect of the community does she need to take into account when planning her intervention?

Conclusion

The ways children learn to express and deal with aggression are complex. These aggression-related patterns of behaviour become established as part of the ways children form themselves into groups and take roles in those groups. Both individual differences and the ethos of particular schools are important. It is possible to describe different patterns of aggression at different ages and for schools to devise and implement programmes to reduce aggression and increase co-operative behaviour between children. The social nature of bullying raises questions about the adult culture. During adolescence, children are learning how to deal with the adult culture, as well as the social effects of schools as institutions. Maybe it is a core responsibility of that adult culture to define what it is expecting the children to learn in terms of dealing with aggression in social relationships and to give some protection to the young whilst they are learning it. Are we too embarrassed to admit to the role of aggression and assertion in adult relationships? Are we too close to it to see it, or are the dominant members of our adult society more or less unconsciously allowing dealing with bullying to become an unacknowledged rite of passage to effective membership of adult society?

Some questions to think about

- What influences arising from school experiences might be shaping the relationships between girls and boys in late adolescence?
- Should learning to be less aggressive and more assertive become part of the national curriculum in Citizenship?
- Should children with special needs spend more time on anti-bullying programmes than other children?
- How can inclusive schools best incorporate anti-bullying approaches as a part of their work on creating an inclusive culture?
- Should parenting programmes include material to stress the importance of early independence and assertiveness in children?
- Should adults ignore dominance hierarchies in children?

Chapter 3

How much bullying? Assessment and measurement

For the class teacher, part of the problem of bullying in school is the common dilemma of how to react in a realistic way to pupils' complaints of being victimised. This means in a way which maintains the school's intentions of minimising bullying, but which does not run the risk of maximising a minor complaint into a major incident. Most caretakers, parents as well as teachers, know that on occasions some children complain too much and some too little, and that often a change in behaviour by the complainant can go some way to avoiding victimisation. Indeed, the previous chapter has reviewed some of the evidence which describes how children get better at dealing with inappropriate or unreasonable aggression as they get older, as a normal part of child development. Consequently, a common response is non-committal advice to 'stay out of their way, then'. On the other hand, most teachers know well that some vulnerable children find it impossible to avoid the bully's attentions successfully, because they will be sought out to act as the butt of the aggression. These children very definitely need help. When responding to bullying, teachers face a number of dilemmas, such as:

- How can the teacher find the right way to respond on the instant, consistently and in a way that is a part of the normal disciplinary and supportive stance?
- What should be seen as bullying? Should all aggression towards a few known victims be seen as bullying? Should the incident complained about have happened at least once before? Should physical violence have to be involved? Should repeated threats or social exclusion also qualify as bullying?
- What would my colleagues and head of year consider bullying? Will they back me up if this particular situation blows up in any

way? What does the pastoral care management group consider as bullying?

These questions should be answered through the school's anti-bullying policy. The policy should make it clear, in child-friendly terms, what the school considers as bullying. It should also include guidelines for teacher action, including the point at which parents should be contacted.

Teachers recognise certain differences between bullying situations – for example, the group bullying situation or the individual bully; the bullying where the victim does nothing except suffer and the bullying where the victim fights back, sometimes with escalating consequences; and, very commonly, the bullying which seems to consist purely of threats and the bullying where violence is involved. Most bullying seems to be same-sex bullying, but occasionally boys do get involved in systematic violence or threats against certain girls, or vice versa. Duncan (1999) paints a picture of sexual bullying that is intimately related to the way the pupil culture of a particular school provides a structure for the learning of gender relationships. Hence, the teacher's response to the particular bullying instance has to take this whole area of development into account.

In many schools, students involved in bullying may come from minority ethnic groups, or one of the parties may come from an ethnic minority group. What does bullying mean in this context? Should it be seen as a racist incident, or should it be dealt with as a bullying incident? This is highly relevant, especially following the conclusions of the McPherson report into the death of Stephen Lawrence. The report recommends that a much more rigorous approach is required in schools to both teachers' cultural awareness and to monitoring racist harassment and bullying.

Other important aspects of most bullying complaints are the place where it happens, and the particular group of children doing the bullying. Did it happen in the playground, where aggressive horseplay is not at all uncommon, or in the classroom, which should be a purposeful learning environment? Should bullying attract greater sanctions to stop it if it occurs in the classroom? If it occurs outside school, say on the way home, is that still a concern for the school? Should the bullying incident be treated less seriously if the bully appears to be a child who has not been involved in previous aggression, or if the child acting as the bully has previously taken a minor part in earlier bullying incidents with other children as victims? Should the bullying be taken less seriously, or more seriously, if it is 'bullying by proxy', where, for example, one girl orders others to exclude a classmate from their friendship groups? Part of the uncertainty faced by the teacher in the corridor or the parent at home is not knowing how important these background factors are, and having the space and support to evaluate earlier decisions based on past practice.

To be able to make such decisions quickly, and communicate them reasonably to others involved, teachers and other staff need to know how important these factors are and how they influence each other. A clear understanding of the meaning of the term by all concerned, particularly by all those concerned inside a particular school, is crucial. As the views of bullying usually vary, it is essential that all the members of the school community discuss the issues for long enough to come to their own clear consensus of what bullying is. The main variables are age, gender and the role played by the particular child in the bullying process, but other factors, such as power imbalance, provocation, persistence, and age difference, will be discussed as well. These discussions in each school or community are also likely to establish that many different types of bullying can be recognised.

Defining the nature of bullying

The word 'bullying' is used freely in popular publications and it is a term, like the word 'intelligence' which seems well understood in terms of common meaning by the general public, in the United Kingdom at least. Unlike the word 'intelligence', there have not been many academic attempts at defining it, although it is likely that there will be as much diversity of interpretation as there has been for 'intelligence'.

Researchers' definitions of bullying

Heinemann (1973) was one of the first researchers to draw attention to bullying. Working in Sweden, he called the activity *møbbning* (i.e., 'mobbing'). In both the English and Swedish language this word limits the process to an action started and carried out by a group. His description of 'mobbing' as group violence against a deviant individual, which occurs suddenly and also subsides suddenly, was conceptually related to studies of animal and bird behaviour. This makes sense if one does not try to see it as exactly equivalent to bullying amongst children, as the term is more widely understood.

Olweus used a wider definition, which at first assumed that only boys bullied: 'A bully is a boy who fairly often oppresses or harasses somebody else; the target may be boys and girls, the harassment physical or mental' (Olweus 1978: 35). With this, he introduced the notion of there being a psychological aspect to bullying. This broadens the definition considerably and also makes it more difficult to describe in observable terms. Since Olweus' work was published, most other researchers have also included 'psychological' or 'mental' as well as physical actions in their definitions – for example 'The long-term and systematic use of violence, mental or physical, against an individual who is unable to defend himself in an actual situation' (Roland in Besag 1989: 3). This author also introduces a new feature, stressing a long-term and systematic aspect to the actions described as bullying. Not all authors would see these as necessary elements. It could, for instance, be argued that one physical attack or threat to an individual who is powerless might make that person feel frightened, restricted or upset over a considerable length of time, both because of the emotional trauma following such an attack and also due to the fear of renewed attacks. It would therefore be more precise to consider that it is possibly the *lasting* or *long-term effect* on the victim rather than the systematic or repeated nature of the action/threat that is the more essential feature of bullying. However, on the other hand, one could argue that the long-term aspect of bullying relates, not only to repeated actions taking place, but also to a stable, pathological system of interpersonal interaction that is persistent and resistant to change. Such a view also includes another new element, the inability of the victim to defend him/herself in the bullying situation. This suggests a power dimension. As we have seen, Bjørkvist *et al.*, writing in Scandinavia, took this a step further by emphasising the social aspects of bullying, as well as the contexts in which it most often takes place:

> We view bullying as a special case of aggression, which is social [in] its nature. It appears only in relatively small social groups (such as school classes and army units), the members of which see each other regularly, usually daily.
>
> (Bjørkqvist *et al.* 1982: 23)

A one-to-one bullying interaction does not happen in isolation. It has an effect on the group, whilst the group has an effect on the subsequent bullying interactions. These social effects are important elements of the best definitions of bullying. Besag introduced a further dimension, which could be seen as the 'moral' definition of bullying, in the following:

> Bullying is a behaviour which can be defined as the repeated attack – physical, psychological, social or verbal – by those in a position of power, which is formally or situationally defined, on those who are powerless to resist, with the intention of causing distress for their own gain or gratification.
>
> (Besag 1989: 4)

Olweus (1978) devised a questionnaire for pupils in order to measure the incidence of bullying. He prefaced his questionnaire by a definition, which was more extensive than the earlier one quoted. For the Sheffield/DfEE anti-bullying project (Smith and Sharp 1994), this definition was translated and also slightly modified. It was then used as a preface to the fully translated Olweus questionnaire and to establish the incidence of bullying in schools in Sheffield:

> We say a young person is being bullied, or picked on, when another child or young person, or a group of children or young people, say nasty and unpleasant things to him or her. It is also bullying when a young person is hit, kicked, threatened, locked inside a room, sent nasty notes, when no-one ever talks to them and things like that. These things can happen frequently and it is difficult for the young person being bullied to defend himself or herself. It is also bullying when a young person is teased repeatedly in a nasty way. But it is not bullying when two young people of about the same strength have the odd fight or quarrel.
>
> (Whitney and Smith 1993: 7)

This definition does not specifically mention the aspects of power, intentionality and motivation, which were included by some of the other authors, although it could be claimed that these are implied by the activities quoted. Nor does it include the emphasis on the social dimension. It is thus clear from the above that, whilst there is a considerable overlap between the various definitions used and quoted, there is also a variation in emphasis and, sometimes, in essentials.

A legal definition of bullying

In the first legal case of its kind, a combined definition was used to decide on whether a girl had been bullied. The judge in this case decided that, for legal purposes, he needed a definition that included intent, but also observable actions. He eventually used a combination of the definitions used by Roland (1989a) and by Tattum (1993):

> Bullying is long-standing violence, physical or psychological, conducted by an individual or group and directed against an individual who is not able to defend himself in the actual situation with a conscious desire to hurt, threaten or frighten that individual or put him under stress.
>
> (Heald 1994: 3)

What is common to all the above definitions is that these are based on the various authors' opinions on what constitutes bullying. Later on, these definitions have been used to collect further data on the incidence of bullying. This is often done by asking children questions using the term 'bullying', and is sometimes supported by a written definition of what the researcher means by the term. When the researcher defines bullying idiosyncratically, the results can be difficult to interpret in comparison with other research. Take, for instance, the case of a school in which one wishes to find out the extent of bullying. It will be unclear to the staff which definition of bullying to use when starting a dialogue with their pupils. Should they use one that emphasises the difference in power between the parties involved? Should intention be part of the definition? Should one ignore those aspects and quote the longer one by Whitney and Smith (1993)? Or maybe combine them all? Achieving a brief but comprehensive definition which is clear to all concerned, especially children, is easier said than done, particularly where it is created by a group of people as a part of their school policy. Box 3.1 gives an illustration of how one school managed this process.

There are two further problems with the use of a definition chosen from the literature to gather information about the incidence of bullying in a school. First, it would not necessarily express what these particular teachers, parents or children really thought was bullying. Second, research has shown that if one does use a pre-set definition at the beginning of a questionnaire or interview, the contents of this may easily be forgotten by the time the questions are being answered

(Arora 1996a). Thus, when asked whether they have been bullied, children may answer from their own previously held reference point, rather than with the initially given definition in mind.

Young people's definitions of bullying and those of their teachers

The word 'bullying' is used to denote a wide variety of actions which may have different motivations, different types of outcomes for the victim and for the perpetrator, and different types of aggression. Tattum and Herbert (1997) propose five forms of bullying: physical bullying, verbal bullying, gesture bullying, extortion bullying and exclusion bullying. The present authors have found these categories a useful starting point in discussions with teachers and pupils in schools. Others have made a distinction between direct and indirect bullying. The understanding of the concept of indirect bullying varies, however, between researchers, from incidents which do not involve direct physical aggression, such as verbal bullying (Lagerspetz *et al.* 1988; Bjørkqvist *et al.* 1992) or exclusion bullying (Olweus 1991), to those actions which are carried out by others, at the bully's behest.

Further evidence for the variability in defining bullying comes from young people themselves. When young people in one secondary school were provided with a long and varied list of specific bullying-type actions, such as hitting, kicking, calling names, demanding money, etc., and then were asked what else they would call bullying, about half of them added further comments (Arora and Thompson 1987). Content analysis of these comments led to twelve different types of constructs or dimensions generated by the pupils. Table 3.1 shows the results. It can be seen that the young people, as a group, were able to generate a sophisticated model of bullying, with about 60 per cent of the constructs used relating to physical aggression (either direct or threatened), and just under a third relating to other types of aggression. Their teachers responded to the list in almost the same way. Smith and Levan (1995), in their study of bullying amongst 6-year-olds, found a similar range of constructs mentioned, even at that age, with 70 per cent of pupils including direct physical examples, 45 per cent including direct verbal examples and 15 per cent including indirect examples.

Table 3.1 Frequency of elements included in the definition of bullying provided by 13 to 14-year-olds

	Year 9		Year 10			
	Boys	Girls	Boys	Girls	Total	
Number of respondents (Total n = 284)	44	51	26	34	145	

Elements mentioned	Frequency of mention					Percentage of responses
Direct physical aggression	18	24	8	8	58	40
Group vs. single person	11	15	9	9	44	30
Frequency	11	9	5	3	28	14
Taunting*	2	12	2	5	21	14
Picking on someone	4	10	3	3	20	14
For no reason	5	3	3	3	14	10
Threats of physical aggression	8	3	2	6	19	13
Older vs. younger	3	6	3	3	15	>1
At one remove	1	5	1	4	11	7
Attempt to elicit fight	5	4	1	0	10	7
Allegations about self/family	2	4	1	3	10	7
Taking possessions	4	3	1	0	8	6
Total number of elements mentioned	74	98	39	47	258	

Notes
* 'Taunting' includes: making fun/teasing/swearing/asking rude or personal questions

Physical aggression as the main component in the definition of bullying

The evidence quoted above suggests that, as a group, young people of all ages generate a wide range of actions that may be related to bullying. As a group, they seem as sophisticated as researchers in their recognition of the variety of actions that could be seen as bullying (Rigby 1996).

One question that the research cannot answer at present is the ways in which younger children's ideas of bullying are different from those of older children. The question 'Are you being bullied?' is highly likely to have a different meaning if asked of 6-year-olds than if the same question was posed to 12-year-olds. Evidence that there may be an age factor comes from Madsen (1997). She notes that none of her sample of primary school children, and only a very small proportion of secondary school children, spontaneously cited bullying as a psychological attack. Arora and Thompson (1987) provided pupils in three age-groups (12, 13 and 14) with a list of the unfriendly items of the 'Life in School' checklist (Arora 1994, see Appendix). They found that there were six items which were consistently more often perceived as bullying by all the three secondary age-groups which were surveyed, as well as by their teachers (Table 3.2). More than half of all pupils agreed that if these things happened to them, they would call it bullying. Smith (1991), using the same checklist in a large survey of Wolverhampton primary schools, found the same six, with an even higher percentage of young people agreeing that these were bullying. In Greece, using a translated version of the same checklist, Kalliotis (1994) identified the same six items in his survey of 11 to 12-year-olds. This suggests that a high agreement exists amongst children regardless of age, about certain actions being included in the term 'bullying'.

However, it should also be noted from Table 3.2 that such actions are all related to physical aggression, either direct, threatened or implicit. None of the actions relate to the more psychological or indirect types of bullying. These types, such as name-calling, frightening someone, etc., were included in the list, but were nominated as being bullying by a far smaller percentage of young people. Such activities are relatively common among young people as parts of other, less intentionally aggressive, patterns of interaction. This includes rough-and-tumble play or practical jokes amongst friends. They may not therefore typically be seen by children as a form of bullying.

There is further evidence for a persistent tendency to equate bullying with physical aggression. In an interview study in which

Table 3.2 Items from the Life in School checklist identified as bullying by 12 to 14-year-old respondents

By 40–70% of respondents	By less than 30% of respondents
Tried to hurt me	Called me names
Threatened to hurt me	Tried to frighten me
Demanded money from me	Asked me for some money
Tried to break something of mine	Laughed at me
Tried to hit me	Took something off me
Tried to kick me	Threatened to tell on me

Source: Arora (1994)

15-year-old boys were asked whether there was much bullying going on in their schools (Thompson and Arora 1991), the majority of the boys reacted initially by saying that there was no bullying in their school. However, when they were subsequently asked whether there was any verbal bullying, they were all able to quote evidence of this. This happened despite them having been presented, only a few minutes earlier, with a wide definition of what bullying was, with examples of verbal and non-verbal types of bullying as a start to the interview.

This does not mean that children would not accept that there are other types of bullying as well. Young people may make more sophisticated decisions if they are aware of the total context, sequence and consequence of a bullying interaction and recognise also more subtle actions as bullying. If interventions are going to work, however, then the diversity of understanding of bullying should clearly be recognised, and the interventions linked clearly to specific kinds of bullying. If the interventions are not targeted at the specific types of bullying for which they were designed, it is highly unlikely they will be effective. There are a number of reasons for this, which are discussed below.

One possible consequence of a tendency to equate bullying with physical aggression is that any study that asks, 'Are you being bullied?' will tap mostly those actions that are related to physical aggression. This should be kept in mind when reading the next main section in this chapter, which considers the research on the incidence of bullying. However, despite the variation in the definitions of bullying, it is possible to conclude that bullying behaviour has, at its centre, the following characteristics:

- The behaviour is persistent and systematic (i.e., the same people behave in the same way in repeated situations).
- The behaviour induces fear in the victim.
- The behaviour is based on an imbalance or abuse of power.
- The behaviour usually takes place in a group context.

Finding out about the extent of bullying

Issues to consider

The previous section has shown that there is not one clear, generally accepted or widely agreed definition of bullying across all stakeholders of children, parents, school staff, researchers and the general public.

Typically, the definition varies according to the purposes of the user, usually omitting some of the features of the meaning seen as important by others. Yet, it is vital for particular communities that the extent of bullying is identified and monitored, as this is an important index of the emotional atmosphere of the community, whether it is a school or a wider group. Good and reliable information will indicate whether bullying is indeed a problem significant enough to need attention. An effective measuring tool can assist a school, initially with tackling the problem and, subsequently, with assessing the effectiveness of its intervention.

The research literature does not provide details of the number of bullying incidents in any particular school over a period of time. The main reason for this is that it is very rare for schools to keep such records in a systematic way, due to variability in definitions used amongst staff and lack of attention to keeping records in this degree of detail in the pastoral care and discipline systems in general. This lack of attention to keeping long-term statistics is probably related to the lack of review systems for anti-bullying policies which would use such statistics if they were available. There are, however, a number of other ways in which researchers have assessed the incidence of bullying, using mainly two approaches. The first approach is to break down the concept of bullying into a number of different bullying-type behaviours, without using the word 'bullying' at all. Respondents are then asked about the incidence of such behaviours happening (Arora and Thompson 1987). The second approach is to define first what bullying is and then ask the respondents about the extent to which this took place (Olweus 1978). There have also been combinations of the two approaches. A third way, exemplified by Cole (1977) and Smith and Sharp (1994) is to ask the teachers about what bullying occurs in their classes or school. This is often done in conjunction with the other methods.

After early surveys using teacher reports only (Lowenstein 1978; Stephenson and Smith 1989), most studies have taken pupils' own reports as the main source of information. Such an approach was warranted by findings that teachers tended to underestimate the amount of bullying taking place, as they were often not witnesses to such events, were not told by pupils that such events took place and may have been using a different definition of bullying from that used by their pupils. Surveys have asked the pupils either whether they were bullied themselves, or whether they saw someone else being bullied, or whether they had bullied someone. There is thus information available on the number of incidents which pupils reported they were subjected to, on the number of times pupils felt they were bullied or had bullied someone else, and on the number of times that pupils had seen others being bullied.

The incidence of bullying

The question that has been asked most often is about the incidence of bullies and victims. In 1977 Olweus used a questionnaire to gather evidence from 1,000 boys aged 13 and 15 in an entire Norwegian district. They were asked whether they had been bullied during the last week, the last month and the last term. They were also asked whether they themselves had bullied others during these periods. Olweus suggested, on the basis of his findings, that 5 per cent of these boys had been seriously bullied and a further 5 per cent had been bullied, but not as seriously. He also identified a similar percentage of perpetrators of serious and less-serious bullying. As he found little overlap between victims and bullies he estimated that, on average, one in five children was likely to be either bullied or a bully. This figure is often quoted in media publications.

Since then, Olweus' questionnaire has been used in many countries, not only with boys, but with girls, too. Olweus himself used the questionnaire in Norway in 1993 with boys (n = 42,324) and girls (n = 40,887) in the 5–16 age-group. On this occasion, 3 per cent of children reported being bullied once a week and 7–8 per cent 'now and then'. Similarly, 2 per cent of children confessed to bullying once a week, with 9 per cent 'now and then'. The figures vary considerably from country to country. For instance, in the UK, Whitney and Smith (1993) conducted a survey in the same year as Olweus, with an 8–16 age-group (n = 6,000). They obtained higher percentages: 2–7 per cent of children reported being bullied at least once a week and 6–15 per cent 'now and then'; 5–8 per cent confessed to bullying at least once a week and 13–29 per cent 'now and then'. This figure is even higher in Southern European countries (Genta *et al.* 1996). When a similar questionnaire was given to a large group of youngsters aged 9–17 in Australia (Rigby 1996), 16.9 per cent reported being bullied at least once a week. In Canada, Bentley and Li (1995) report an incidence of 21.3 per cent of children being bullied and 11.6 per cent bullying others.

The 'Life in School' checklist (Arora and Thompson 1987) was developed to provide information about how often pupils have been subjected to different types of bullying behaviour, in a form simple enough for schools to use and adapt for their own needs (Arora 1994; 1996b). Its main purpose is for a school to be able to gauge the amount of bullying taking place, based on specific incidents but without mentioning the word 'bullying'. This avoids the confounding issue of people's different concepts of bullying. It is translated easily into other languages (cf. Kalliotis 1994) and used in other cultures (Nabuzoka 1999). It can also be easily adapted to different needs (Smith 1991) and is quick to administer. For those who wish to maintain the word 'bullying' as a meaningful term, it provides the possibility of calculating a Bullying Index. This is based on responses that indicate that a young person has been subject to certain actions *more than once* during the previous week. At present, the Bullying Index is used by the authors in an exploratory and descriptive way, as the various schools using the Life in School booklet provide only a little information about their natural ranges and variability. The Index forms what statisticians call an 'ordinal' measure, which means it can be used to make statements about greater or lesser amounts, but cannot be used to calculate averages. The Index is, however, an inherently meaningful descriptor statistic to give very rapid summaries for purposes of year-to-year comparisons inside particular schools.

Some of the bullying-type actions, without any context, could be interpreted as not really being bullying. However, two-thirds of those who reported that the actions in the left-hand column of Table 3.2 (see p. 57) had happened to them more than once during the previous week also confirmed that they had been 'bullied' the previous week. This suggests that the basic premise of the checklist – i.e. that it provides an estimate of bullying, based on children's perceptions – is valid.

Whilst the checklist was not developed specifically to estimate the incidence of bullying for large numbers of pupils, it has been used extensively. Figures are now available, expressed in terms of a Bullying Index, from a large number of schools. Further information about how to use the Life in School checklist can be found in the Appendix. This also contains findings from UK primary and secondary schools and a case study of how one secondary school came to use the checklist. For primary schools, the Bullying Index is usually significantly lower than for secondary schools. A wide variation between schools is found when they calculate the Bullying Index, regardless of size or type of school. This is similar to other findings: Olweus (1978) did not find any significant differences between the number of bullies and victims identified in terms of size of schools, size of classes, or whether these were town or rural schools; in the Sheffield/DfEE project, no relationship was found between school size and extent of bullying (Whitney and Smith 1993). Only Stephenson and Smith (1989) report consistent differences between small and large, and between town and rural, schools.

Long-term bullying

This has been a relatively neglected aspect of bullying research. Cole (1977) in a study of teacher views of bullying carried out during the summer term found that many teachers felt that the bullying relationships they knew of in their classrooms had been established before the children had come into their classes in the previous September. This would mean they had existed for at least eight to twelve months. Rigby and Slee (1993) investigated this in their Australian research. They found that approximately 8 per cent of children had been bullied for at least six months. Thompson (1995) followed up the incidence of bullying in the secondary schools which had been involved in the Sheffield/DfEE anti-bullying project (Smith and Sharp 1994) and, in a specific question: 'How long have you been bullied?', found that from a whole-school survey of five large secondary schools, on average 6 per cent of children reported being bullied for 'all this year' and for 'more than one year' (range: 4–8 per cent across the five schools). Of these, an average of 4 per cent said they had been bullied for more than one year (range: 3–6 per cent). Even the school that had implemented its bullying policies most rigorously, and achieved the lowest overall incidence of bullying amongst the five by a margin of 7 per cent of the school population, still had 4 per cent of children reporting being bullied for more than one year.

Overall, these figures are depressingly consistent and indicate that a large number of children are stuck in the victim role, with possibly the same children acting as bullies, for a long period of time. For a school with a roll of about a thousand, this means fifty children in school being bullied for more than one year. Researchers asking similar questions in the future should extend their horizons: How many children are being bullied for more than two years? These time frames in the life of most children in their early adolescence must seem like forever. How much stress and harm does this bullying cause? How can we quantify such stress?

Age and gender factors

It has already been noted above that of the schools using the Life in School checklist, secondary schools tended to have a lower Bullying Index than primary schools. This implies that there is less bullying in secondary schools than in primary ones. Such a decline in bullying with increased age has been consistently documented. Olweus (1993) reports on the Norwegian nationwide study of primary and secondary schools, carried out in 1983, which analysed the data of 10 per cent of 140,000 pupils aged 8–17. In primary schools, the percentage of victims declined with increasing age, for both boys and girls. By the time they reached the first year of the secondary school, at age 13, boy victims continued to decline, but less steeply. For girls, there was a steep decline from age 12 to age 13 – i.e. when they transferred to the secondary school – after which a steady decline continued. This decline in bully victims with age is similar whether one takes only those who reported being bullied once a week or also includes those who said they were being bullied 'now and then' (Roland 1989). In Australia, where there is also a transfer to secondary education at 13 years, being bullied increased markedly at this point, but was followed by an increasing decline, similar to the Norwegian findings. In the UK, Whitney and Smith (1993) noted a similar decline in being bullied with increased age.

Assessing how many pupils bully others is not as clear-cut. Pupils may be less inclined to confess to a disapproved activity such as bullying, even if the questionnaires are anonymous. This could affect the total response rate to and possibly the validity of a survey. In the Norwegian study, Olweus found slightly fewer pupils who admitted to being bullies than to being bullied. There was a gender factor, with boys admitting much more frequently to having bullied than girls, especially in the secondary age-group (13–17). Girls reported having bullied less frequently with increasing age.

In discussing the incidence of bullying with respect to girls, one of the factors that may be complicating the estimations of incidence is a possible overlap with aspects of sexual harassment. Duncan (1999) and others have illustrated how the emerging relationships between boys and girls in secondary schools can be unduly influenced by aggression and power relationships. It would be perfectly possible for girls subjected to undue verbal aggression from boys in schools, or vice versa, to see such relationships as aspects of growing up which are to be expected. Alternatively, if they find themselves taking part in a survey, they may see it as unreasonable behaviour which should be classed as bullying. The incidence of bullying reported in that school would be different depending on how the pupils defined what was happening to them. For example, factors such as how explicit the definition of bullying was in the school's anti-bullying policy, whether the school had any kind of sexual harassment policy specific enough to influence how pupils interpreted their treatment, or how energetically the anti-bullying policy was being implemented, would be likely to influence how much bullying occurred.

Much the same situation of overlap with other forms of aggression applies with regard to racism in schools. In theory, the researcher's definition of bullying – of a group bullying a single individual over a period of time – may include instances which others would categorise as racism if the victim were a member of a minority community (Gillborn 1990). If the main intention in selecting a victim was the humiliation of a member of the minority community, with the associated rejection of that community, this categorisation is perfectly justified. On the other hand, it is also possible that the selection of this particular victim had nothing to do with his or her ethnicity. It may well be that bullying where the victim is a member of a minority community is much more heavily suppressed by staff in some schools precisely because of its racist nature, and has a lower frequency of occurrence for this reason (Thompson and Arora 1991). These overlaps, and the possibility of multiple categorisations, confuse the question: 'how much bullying is going on?', except in the very simple judgement of: 'it's not getting out of hand', or 'too much'.

Theoretical differences between bullying, racial harassment and sexual harassment

From the point of view of the victim, all three of these systematic forms of aggression will feel similar – the psychological impact of each form of harassment is to reduce the self-esteem and self-confidence of the victim by a variety of means. This is true whatever meaning the harassing activity has in the eyes of the aggressor. There may be certain differences between the psychological processes of all three, which may have some relevance for the response of the institution. Specifically, we do not know that the incidence of all three is reduced by the same intervention methods: what evidence we have suggests otherwise – for example, that racial name-calling is not reduced by anti-bullying policies themselves (Smith and Sharp 1994). At present, these three aspects of aggressive harassment have not been investigated systematically together, only as separate phenomena, except in Duncan's (1999) interpretative account of 'sexual bullying'. They clearly involve similar overt behaviour on the part of the aggressors, and similar experiences of victimisation and humiliation on the part of the victims. Racial harassment is explicitly based on membership of minority ethnic groups, where the aggressor is from a different group to the victim. It may also have elements of territoriality and of access to resources, at least as far as the community backing for the discrimination is concerned. It also relates to one of the psychological challenges of adulthood – how to relate to those members of the human race who do not belong to your own community group, who are present in the same town or city, who from time to time may be competing for territory or resources or sexual favours, and who are clearly recognisable by skin colour, dress, religious affiliation or culture. Sexual harassment is also based on real differences and is related to another emerging challenge to personality development – how to relate to members of the other gender. It also involves learning the use of aggression or assertion in establishing continuing relationships.

'Homophobic bullying' is often not what it appears to be, in schools at least. Duncan (1999) demonstrates in graphic detail how the word 'gay' is used as a general epithet meaning 'weak' and not conforming to the usual 'macho' standards of behaviour expected from adolescent boys. It was not used to suggest that the victim had homosexual tendencies in any real sense. One of his informants even went out of his way to emphasise that such name-calling did not mean he had got anything personal against his target of the abuse; 'gay' was just a general word of abuse, to be used against anyone who was to be excluded from the dominant groupings amongst the boys. Clearly, when genuine homophobic bullying does occur, it is likely to be particularly hurtful and damaging. Much school bullying cannot be assumed to be homophobic in the ordinary sense, except in that it reflects an adolescent culture where 'gay' is assumed to be a generally derogatory insult. This in itself would further increase the sense of rejection and stigmatisation for children attempting to clarify or come to terms with a different sense of sexuality.

In practice, such distinctions may help in thinking through exactly what kind of cultural change is needed, but the bigger challenge is making the change in that culture of aggression and victimisation in reality. Rivers (1996; 2000a; 2000b) has extended our understanding of the experiences of adolescents who suffered homophobic bullying whilst they were at school through retrospective studies, and also demonstrates some of the implications for schools in terms of absenteeism and exclusion. In general, his findings seem to indicate that young people who see themselves as gay suffer from bullying more frequently than those able to identify with the heterosexual majority. He also suggests that schools can make some difference to levels of bullying by using general anti-bullying strategies. Rivers notes that these pupils should be considered as one of the groups of young people more vulnerable to bullying and to the negative consequences of bullying for personality development and school achievement.

Racial and sexual harassment develop much of their power during and following adolescence, but bullying is more common during the primary school years than at secondary level. It is possible that the 'social skills' of bullying developed in the primary phase may find their expression in racial and sexual harassment at secondary level, as well as in the continuation of the 'ordinary' bullying in a reduced, but possibly more specific, way. Such a hypothesis would need some longitudinal research to follow it up: do those identified as showing bullying behaviour at primary school become the adolescents who show tendencies to become involved in racial and sexual harassment? Such a relationship would have some logical support: the expectation of gaining social status from systematic aggression, and the skills of exclusion and humiliation of victims and manipulation of significant members of a peer group do not occur in all children. If such behaviours become established at primary level they would persist in adolescence. This means that early intervention is important, and also that that intervention should include developing constructive social skills (prosocial skills).

Implications for researchers of this variability in the definition of bullying

These dilemmas discussed above, of how far it is useful to extend the term 'bullying' without qualification of the nature of the psychological processes underlying the behaviour – illustrate well some of the thinking behind Arora's (1996b) arguments. She claims that for the purposes of clarification of the details of the bullying processes, researchers need to be sure to describe the various constituent elements in the behaviour generally described as bullying. They need to relate the emerging theory to the development and expression of these constituent behaviours rather than to one general concept of bullying itself. In a nutshell, she would say that the differences in interpretation of the word between all the stakeholders involved, as well as the intense dependence of the process on the particular social situation of each individual child, mean that future research which bases its description and theory on one general concept of 'bullying' will be unlikely to add much to the sum of current knowledge. It is very unlikely that the word will become redundant, either in common parlance or as a generic word for researchers, but it is likely that with time and increasing sophistication of research, more specific patterns of bullying behaviour will come to be the subject of the enquiries. When used in an unqualified way by researchers, the safest definition for readers to assume is the relatively 'pure' one of repeated 'mobbing', where a group of bullies with a definite leader systematically, over a long period of time, demonstrates domination over an individual victim who cannot defend him or herself, irrespective of whether this particular bullying has a racist, sexist or homophobic basis.

However, as a description of a 'marker' pattern of behaviour that is highly likely to be related to other forms of group and individual aggression in schools, assessing the incidence of bullying is still very often the first serious action in the attempt to minimise such aggressive patterns. School staff and parents are usually well aware of the other kinds of aggression occurring in schools, and concentrate on reducing bullying rather than other kinds of aggression only because there appear to be well-defined methods of assessing the extent of the bullying behaviour and of attempting to reduce it. Reducing 'simple' bullying as an organisational goal is potentially a clear, direct process, which usually gains political support from all members of a school community, and has verified means both of achieving the reductions and of assessing the impacts of those programmes. The theoretical ambiguity of categorising a general group of systematic aggressive relationships under one head as 'bullying' does not detract from that clarity in practice. It does, however, underline the need to use brief and clear definition for practical purposes in the assessment instruments used and in the policy statements made to clarify policy implementation, in order to minimise potential ambiguities.

Box 3.1 Case study: initiating an anti-bullying policy at Underham Junior School

Underham Junior School is in a small industrial town in a semi-rural area with about 300 pupils on its roll. Its intake is mixed, with about half of the children from the local council estate and others from owner-occupied houses. About 20 per cent of the intake are children from ethnic minorities, mainly from the Asian subcontinent. The staff includes nine to ten teachers and a number of support assistants.

When the headteacher and staff decided to draw up an anti-bullying policy for the school, they were aware that this was going to be a process which would take time and needed a great deal of discussion amongst the stakeholders in the school. In fact, the first thing to do was to draw up a list of these stakeholders. These were: the governors, headteacher, teachers, non-teaching staff (including teacher assistants, administrative assistants, lunchtime supervisors and caretaker), pupils, parents, LEA support staff and local community. Some concern was expressed that such a wide-ranging discussion might create the impression that bullying was a huge problem in the school, but it was acknowledged that this may well become the case if they were not all involved from the start. The initial phase, though, would involve only the immediate stakeholders: the pupils, staff and parents. The deputy head acted as a co-ordinator, forming a small working group and acting as a liaison with the others.

The first question raised with the staff was: what behaviours do we wish to define as bullying behaviours in our school? Discussion amongst the staff revealed that there were a number of differences in emphasis but they were able to decide on a common definition. The next step was to ask the children. This was done through a classroom discussion held during Circle Time (see Chapter 6). The definitions from each class were compared, and a common definition was produced, which also included examples of bullying behaviour. Particular care was taken to refer also to instances of racial harassment and sexual harassment. The statement was then discussed in a meeting with the parents and the governors and circulated to other stakeholders. After further changes, the final text was as follows:

Bullying is a form of aggressive or intimidating behaviour which is usually hurtful and deliberate; it is often persistent, sometimes continuing for weeks, months or even years and it is difficult for those being bullied to defend themselves. Underlying most bullying behaviours is an abuse of power and a desire to intimidate and dominate. Bullying takes the form of uninvited physical, emotional or verbal abuse. It can be:

- physical – hitting, kicking, taking or damaging belongings;
- verbal – name-calling, insulting, repeated teasing, racist remarks, coercing into acts of stealing or bullying against others;
- emotional – spreading nasty rumours; excluding someone from social groups, gesturing;
- sexual – lifting skirts or pulling trousers down.

Bullying behaviour is very subtle. Once a pupil or a group of pupils have established a bullying relationship with their victim, they may only have to look threatening to reinforce their fearfulness.

This process took nearly a term to achieve but it was an excellent beginning for identifying strategies for the anti-bullying policy.

- What is your definition of bullying?
- Are you sure it is one that is shared or at least understood by all the stakeholders in your school?
- How far have the staff in your school gone in the process of developing an anti-bullying policy?
- Are all new staff made aware of the definition and/or policy when they join the school?

Conclusion

Bullying is a complex phenomenon, but researchers have progressed in ways of estimating the incidence of bullying and the types of activities that can be included in the definition. With greater understanding of the nature of bullying, researchers have begun to understand how it overlaps with other expressions of aggression, and how other aspects of growing up may influence the development of bullying behaviour. With such understanding has come a greater sophistication about the reasons for variations in the incidences of bullying from different situations, and a realisation that schools of similar type and size may have wildly different amounts of bullying. This then leads to a realisation that the most useful application of bullying surveys is to assess how the incidence of bullying is changing inside one school over time: do children see it as getting worse, or getting better?

Some questions to think about

- Do children who bully tend to use only one or two types of bullying, or many different ways?
- Do some types of bullying tend to be more short term or ephemeral, and others more long term and serious?
- How would you test the proposal that different forms of systematic aggression involve the same form of social skills and attitude?
- Does it matter if different agencies, groups of educationists and researchers use different definitions of bullying?
- The Secondary Head Teachers Association in the UK recently gave its definition of bullying, but also added that if a student saw him or herself as being bullied, the staff should act on that assumption, whether or not they agreed with it. Is this a sensible way to proceed?

Chapter 4

The experiences of those who are bullied

Whilst much of the earlier research on bullying focused on the nature and extent of the behaviour, more recent studies have begun to look at the emotional and psychological consequences for either the victim or the bully. There has also been a more substantial degree of investigation into stress amongst children and young people. Some of that research has identified issues arising from friendships and peer relations. This chapter considers the findings of those studies that have explored the impact of bullying itself on pupil well-being as well as those which have identified the impact of stress on children and young people.

What is the impact of bullying on children and young people?

Bullying has been linked with low self-esteem, anxiety, impaired concentration, truancy, depression and suicidal thoughts. Bond *et al.* (2001) have recently confirmed that not only is anxiety associated with victimisation, but that also 'a history of victimisation and poor social relationships predicts the onset of emotional problems in adolescence'. Hawker and Boulton (2000) carried out a meta-analysis of all cross-sectional studies published between 1978 and 1997 that made separate measurements of victimisation and psychological and social adjustment. Psychological and social adjustment was assessed by measures of depression, anxiety, loneliness, global and social self-concepts. They found that the pattern of results strongly suggested that victims of bullying experience more negative feelings and thoughts about themselves than their non-bullied peers. This was the case across both sexes, in all age-groups and from diverse populations. Victims of bullying were consistently found to have low self-esteem, were more lonely and anxious. The strongest relationship they found was between bullying and depression. The authors argue convincingly that the outcomes of this meta-analysis establish unequivocally that bullying has a negative psychological and social impact on children and young people and that researchers should now move on to address some of the more complex questions regarding risk, causation and intervention.

Truancy and bullying

Reid (1989) investigated reasons for truancy and found that 15 per cent of persistent absentees said they had stayed away from school initially because of being bullied and 19 per cent continued to stay away from school because of this. Balding *et al.* (1996) carried out a questionnaire survey of 11,000 11 to 16-year-olds from sixty-five schools. Some of the questions in the survey related to fear of going to school, fear of being bullied and self-esteem. They found that of 4,989 Year 8 students, 21.3 per cent of boys and 28.2 per cent of girls reported that they were sometimes afraid to go to school because of bullying; 2.4 per cent of boys and 3.1 per cent of girls felt this 'very often'. These students reported higher frequencies of illness and disease and generally presented as more anxious. They found that students who did not fear bullying were more satisfied with life, had higher self-esteem, had greater feelings of personal control, felt fit, confident with the opposite sex and were taller. In this study we have no information about actual experiences of being bullied, and therefore it is difficult to know whether their higher levels of anxiety generally also lead to a fear of being bullied or whether their fear of bullying arises from actually being bullied. Pervin and Turner (1994) surveyed 147 13- and 14-year-old students in one secondary school: 77 per cent of the boys and 89 per cent of the girls who had experienced bullying found it either worrying or frightening. Two students had changed schools because of the bullying. Sharp (1997) found that 4 per cent of pupils would truant to prevent bullying re-occurring. This increased to 31 per cent amongst pupils with low self-esteem.

Bullying and self-esteem

As reflected in Hawker and Boulton's meta-analysis, bullying and low self-esteem often go together. Initially, it was assumed that children and young people with low self-esteem attracted bullying but, more recently, it has been recognised that bullying can impact negatively on self-esteem. Olweus (1980) found that students who were persistently bullied were more anxious and insecure than other students, had a negative view of themselves, were often lonely and neglected by peers and generally had low self-esteem. Rigby and Slee (1991) report that bullied students showed slightly lower self-esteem than non-bullied peers, but also note that gender was more associated with variations in self-esteem than was victimisation. Neary and Joseph (1994) investigated self-worth, depression and victimisation in sixty 11- and 12-year-old girls. They found that the girls who had scored more highly on a victimisation scale also reported lower global self-worth and poorer self-perceptions of themselves in relation to academic competence, social relationships, attractiveness and conduct.

Salmivalli (1998) has questioned the interpretation of self-esteem measures, distinguishing between 'healthy' and 'unhealthy' high self-esteem ratings. Healthy self-esteem ratings not only relate to positive view of self but also to acceptance of others, prosocial behaviour and good adjustment. In contrast, 'unhealthy' high self-esteem (or 'defensive egotism') indicates inflated beliefs of superiority that lead to vulnerability in the face of threats and to antisocial and aggressive behaviour. Similarly, Salmivalli points out that some people will give low self-esteem scores because of modesty. Salmivalli found that pupils who bullied others were significantly more likely to be rated, by both self and others, as 'defensive egotists'. Pupils who had genuine, or healthy, self-esteem were more likely to defend victimised pupils than bully or be bullied. Salmivalli found that bullied pupils fell across the self-esteem profiles and concluded that victimisation and self-esteem are not necessarily directly related at all. Sharp (1997) similarly found that pupils with high self-esteem had been bullied as much as pupils with low self-esteem but the negative impact of bullying was greater for those pupils who felt bad about themselves. It is likely, then, that although self-esteem may not be directly linked to bullying experiences it does influence how children feel about them.

Thinking about bullying as a cause of stress

Research into stress is far more developed than research into bullying. This section focuses on some of the key concepts of stress and coping in adolescence that may be helpful in understanding bullying relationships, their consequences and their management.

Definitions of stress have become increasingly sophisticated and interactional, acknowledging that individual differences and contextual factors lead to great variations in how different people respond to and manage the same stressor and that an individual's responses vary also over time and between different situations.

Rice *et al.* (1993) propose a model of stress in adolescence that recognises the interrelation of the number of stressful events, the nature of stressful events and the synchronicity of different stressors with other important developmental events or processes. These are mediated by social support and/or internal resources (self-esteem, coping responses, etc.). They describe stress as arising when there is insufficient 'goodness of fit' between the changes and challenges faced by the young person and the available support and individual coping resources which can be drawn upon in meeting the challenges or change.

In a survey of 1,482 10 to 15-year-olds in Western Australia, Garton and Pratt (1995) found that friendship difficulties were rated as quite stressful (mean 3.9 on a scale where 5 is most stressful), especially amongst the younger students. Silverman *et al.* (1995) interviewed 141 boys and 132 girls who were aged between 7 and 12 years and who attended school in Florida. They did not enquire about stress, rather about worries. The children were asked 'Do you worry about . . .?' and then presented with a particular theme. Two of the themes were friends and classmates. Two very interesting findings emerged. First, the things that worried the youngsters most seriously were the things they had least experience of: war, disasters and personal harm. The highest-frequency experiences, which were mostly socially orientated, caused the least anxiety. In terms of personal relationships, 48.9 per cent of youngsters worried about being picked on and 24.4 per cent worried about being rejected. The second finding to emerge was that there were some distinctions between worries about classmates and worries about friends. Concerns about classmates centred around rejection, exclusion from activities and being ignored. Concerns about friendship were mostly related to the possibility of betrayal – for example, telling a secret. Silverman *et al.* (1995: 682) conclude: 'classmates provide children with a sense of acceptance and belonging, whereas close friendships provide intimacy, loyalty and emotional support.' Bullying behaviour, as it often leads to isolation of the victimised child, undermines both the sense of belonging provided by classmates and the intimacy of close friendships.

Yamamoto *et al.* (1987) administered a questionnaire on perceived stressfulness of events to 1,814 children from six different countries. The questionnaire described twenty life events, and the participants were asked to rate how stressful they thought these experiences would be on a scale of 1 to 7. There was considerable similarity across nationalities in terms of the types of life events identified as stressful and the actual experiences of the young people in the study. Without exception, the experience of parental bereavement was rated as the most stressful experience. 'Being ridiculed in class' was the only item on the questionnaire that could be related to bullying behaviour. The percentage of students reporting that they had experienced this and the median ratings are presented in Table 4.1. It is notable that not only was this widely experienced, it was also perceived as unpleasant.

A more recent and more extensive multi-national study of adolescent 'worries' and their coping strategies is reported in Gibson-Cline (1996). Thirteen nations took part in the study, giving a total sample size of 5,067 13 to 15-year-olds, carefully chosen to represent different socio-economic groupings within the countries taking part. Children from the poorest and most disadvantaged communities were included as well as children from the most affluent and advantaged. The data were collected via an open-ended questionnaire that asked the young people to identify three events that they had found worrying or that had made them feel pressured. They were then asked to describe

Table 4.1 Results from an international study of stressful life events for 'being ridiculed in class'

Nationality	Percentage of students reporting that they have been ridiculed in class	Median rating of stressfulness (where 7 = the most upsetting experience
Egyptian	46.2	6.63
Canadian	66.8	4.25
Australian	57.9	4.67
Japanese	65.7	6.11
Philippines	57.7	6.26
USA (1979 sample)	46.9	5.28
USA (1984 sample)	63.7	4.65

Source: Yamamoto *et al.* (1987)

what they did about this problem; who they liked to help them; what qualities this person would have and how he or she would help. The data were coded and analysed to produce 102 categories of problem, 37 classes of coping strategies, 42 types of desired helper, 390 types of desired helper qualities and 27 modes of helping. 'Relationships with peers' was identified as a concern by 6.9 per cent of advantaged females and 8.3 per cent of non-advantaged females.

Branwhite (1994), in a questionnaire survey of 836 11- and 12-year-olds, asked what situations the students found most stressful. Being called names ranked fourth most stressful, below loss of a pet, loss of a relative and going to hospital. Hoover *et al.* (1992) found that of their sample of 207 12- and 18-year-olds, three-quarters had been bullied at some time in their school career and 14 per cent felt that this had been a 'very severe problem' for them. Boulton and Underwood (1992) interviewed 122 8- and 10-year-olds. 80 per cent of those who had experienced bullying reported feeling better about themselves prior to the onset of bullying. Sharp (1997) carried out four linked studies with a total population of 1,131 secondary-aged students. The overall findings of this study suggest that the majority of students who had been bullied, even only once or twice, reported low-level stress. This stress led to mild stress symptoms in many pupils and more severe symptoms in about one in four of bullied pupils. Those students who had been bullied for a term or longer experienced greater stress. The most stressful form of bullying was having nasty rumours spread about self and family. This was consistent across all groups of pupils, regardless of gender, age or ethnicity.

Bullying as a chronic, acute or neutral stressor

Research into stress amongst young people suggests that although other stressors are more disturbing to adolescents, difficulties with peer relationships do cause distress. Trad and Greenblatt distinguish between chronic, acute and neutral stressors. They describe chronic stressors as creating 'an aura or background of stress against which an individual lives, or strives to live, a normal life' (Trad and Greenblatt 1990: 27). Chronic stressors would include long-term illness or disability, socio-economic deprivation, long-term parental arguing (perhaps prior to or following divorce), repeated abuse. The consequences of chronic stress can be positive or negative. Children and young people who experience chronic stressors may experience low self-esteem, depression, anxiety disorders, accident proneness and a decline in general health. Alternatively, they may develop a whole array of coping strategies that actually result in them being more competent at handling adversity and stress in their lives. For example, Emery and Forehand (1994) note that for most children the outcome of parental separation and divorce is increased resilience.

Acute stressors are sudden, brief and intense. They include traumatic incidents, accidents, sudden injury and the immediate impact of divorce or bereavement. These acute stressors often lead to a major change in the child's life for a short period of time. The negative effects of these may include nightmares, 'flashbacks', detachment, sleep disturbances, hypervigilance, anxiety and irritability. Some children who experience acute stressors develop post-traumatic stress disorder. How children perceive their own role in these acute situations will shape the severity of the experience for them. If they perceive themselves as 'triumphing over adversity', their self-esteem can increase and the outcomes can be positive. Both chronic and acute stressors are described as non-normative, in that they are not necessarily part of the usual range of experiences in adolescence.

The final group of stressors identified by Trad and Greenblatt are termed 'neutral'. Other researchers have described them as 'generic' or 'normative' (Compas *et al.* 1993). These are common experiences – 'daily hassles and small events' – that lead to a change in environment or routine, such as moving house, the birth of a sibling or a change of teacher. Whilst most people would perceive the acute and chronic stressors as adverse, neutral stressors are given a positive or negative connotation by the people directly involved. The accumulative effects of these more usual, quite frequent, stressors have been linked to the development of psychological symptoms but not maladjustment or psychopathology (DuBois *et al.* 1992).

These three broad categories of stressor are not mutually exclusive. They can occur together and one type of stressor can lead into another. Compas *et al.* (1993) suggest that chronic daily stress is a mediator between major life events and psychological distress. Both Pearlin (1991) and Rutter (1994) criticise much of the research into stress in adolescence and adulthood for focusing too much on individual stressful events and not considering sufficiently the probability that individuals will usually experience multiple stressors and that these could be interrelated.

What type of stressor is bullying? Whether bullying behaviour is seen as chronic, acute or neutral will depend on how bullying is defined and the nature or severity of the bullying which is experienced. Bullying relationships that persist over time would almost certainly be described as chronic. In this scenario, the child's school life is set against a backdrop of frequent and regular intimidation and threat from peers. One-off incidents of bullying or occasional bullying which cause deep distress or hurt would be classed as acute. Can bullying ever be described as a neutral stressor? Probably not, in so far as it is usually perceived as an unpleasant experience (Sharp 1997). However, if one takes the view that bullying is a common feature of school life, experienced occasionally by many students, then perhaps some types of bullying do fall into the category of 'daily hassles and small events'. However, it is important to remember how large the differences can be between transient, minor acts of bullying and established patterns of bullying relationships which can last for more than a year, as discussed in Chapter 3.

Accumulative stress

Holmes and Rahe (1967) proposed that the general rate of change in a person's life could cause stress leading to illness. On the basis of this, they developed their 'life changes' questionnaire, which provides a summative score reflecting the overall quantity of change and major events. They predict that people who score highly are more likely to suffer the negative effects of stress. Cohen et al. (1987) tested the longitudinal effects of accumulative life events on 312 12- and 13-year-olds from five schools. They also collected data about life events experienced by the students' parents. They found that accumulative negative life events led to an increase in anxiety and depression and a lowering of self-esteem. However, they also found that positive life events reduced the impact of the negative life events. Again these findings are relevant when the persistent nature of bullying behaviour is considered. The balance between nega- tive bullying incidents and other positive events in an individual youngster's life could influence the impact of the bullying behaviour on the young person. Students who are persistently bullied in school and who experience few positive life events could be more at risk of developing psychological and emotional difficulties. The negative impact of bullying will vary according to the extent to which the bullying persists and the balance of other negative and positive events in the individual student's life. This could explain why response to bullying varies from person to person, with some people much more profoundly affected than others.

Immediate and long-term physical responses to stress

The immediate physiological response to stress is universal. When under stress, our bodies prepare for flight or fight through changes in our physical state designed to improve our performance: blood supplies from the stomach, intestines and skin are sent to the brain and heart to improve judgement, decision-making and breathing rate; extra energy is produced by increased release of glucose and fats into the bloodstream; and the sympathetic nervous system activates hormone release mechanisms that produce catecholamines, leading to multi-physiological change. Alternatively, a conservation-withdrawal response is activated by corticoids, leading to helplessness and depression, sometimes called 'frozen watchfulness' (Henry 1980). Whilst occasional stress responses enhance our performance for a short period of time, repeated exposure to stress can lead to permanent structural damage.

As well as actual physiological responses to stress, various psychosomatic symptoms can also develop. Ryan-Wenger (1990) reports a longitudinal examination of services used by 47,145 children in a private health care scheme: 17.3 per cent of diagnoses for children under the age of 11 were classed as psychosomatic. The most frequent forms of psychosomatic symptoms in school-aged children are stomach ache and headache. Ryan-Wenger points out that most psychosomatic medicine is speculative, and there is no real theory or knowledge about why or how these symptoms arise. The most common belief is that the electrochemical neural circuits in the brain that interpret life experiences also influence physiological reactions.

Psychosomatic symptoms have been linked with non-supportive family or social environments, stressful life events and ineffective coping strategies. There is some evidence which suggests that the long-term physiological and psychosomatic effects of persistent daily hassles, such as many forms of bullying, are more significant than major life events and traumas (Lazarus and Folkman, 1984). The development of a psychosomatic symptom can result in more stress and therefore create a vicious cycle. Sears and Milburn (1990) suggest the following list of signs or symptoms of too much stress in school-aged children:

- regression to infantile behaviour: bed-wetting, nail-biting, thumb-sucking;
- uncharacteristic withdrawal: not talking to anyone, appearing depressed;
- loss of motivation or inability to concentrate at school;
- noticeable changes in behaviour;
- poor appetite and sleeplessness;
- unexplained irritability;
- physical ailments: headache, stomach ache;
- trouble getting along with peers.

Studies of the impact of bullying upon health suggest that persistently bullied young people are showing classic symptoms of stress. Rigby and Slee (1993b) found that students who were being bullied 'at least once a week' showed significantly more health problems than non-bullied students, as reported on a general health questionnaire. The bullied students reported higher levels of somatic complaints, general depression and suicidal thoughts. Haselager and Van Lieshout (1992) found that bullied students are more likely to show signs of depressive distress, negative self-evaluations and physical complaints than other classmates are. They were also more likely to be shy and withdrawn and rejected by peers, and less likely to be chosen as a best friend.

Sharp (1997) found that 26 per cent of secondary-aged students who had been bullied felt ill as a result. They also reported difficulties with concentration and sleeping, as well as displaying increased irritability and having flashbacks to the bullying situation.

Individual differences in responses to stress: resilience and vulnerability

Stress researchers have long been interested in the fact that some people face the most adverse conditions and thrive and gain from them, whereas other people in the same situation can be devastated and suffer both short- and long-term negative effects. This interest has led to a large body of research into resilience and vulnerability. Risk factors increase the likelihood of a negative outcome for the individual. Protective factors are attributes of the person, the environment and the situation. These appear to prevent the development of negative outcomes – i.e., they increase resistance to risk or 'buffer' the person against negative stress effects. Resilience is an individual characteristic reflecting the development of highly effective strategies for managing stress. People are usually identified as resilient when they have already demonstrated successful adaptation to stressful events and situations.

Protective factors are usually grouped into two categories:

- personal factors (e.g. physical health, temperament, self-esteem, beliefs about control and competence);
- environmental resources (e.g. family income, attachment to significant others, religious affiliation).

Werner (1989) noted that whilst risk factors are often embedded in culture, protective factors are more universal and less influenced by cultural difference. For children and young people, Garmezy and Masten (1991) postulate that the three most significant protective factors are:

- a positive disposition or personality;
- a supportive family context;
- an external support system that encourages and reinforces successful coping.

Kimchi and Schaffner (1990) propose that whilst constitutional protective factors are more important in childhood, in adolescence it is interpersonal factors, such as locus of control, sense of control over the future and planning to obtain realistic goals, which are crucial.

Werner (1989) monitored the impact of stressful life events on 698 Asian and Polynesian children from birth to age 30. Seventy-two children were identified as resilient and their development was carefully charted. In the primary years the resilient youngsters demonstrated good problem-solving and communication skills, were sociable, flexible and independent. As adolescents they had an internal locus of control, high self-concept and internalised values. They were achievement orientated, socially mature and perceptive and nurturing of others. The autonomy and social orientation of these youngsters was notable from their pre-school year. Werner *et al.* observed that they were adept at recruiting substitute parent figures.

An outgoing, extravert manner is a recurring feature in research into resilience (see Kimchi and Schaffner 1990 for a review). It seems that these resilient youngsters work on establishing good relationships with others, thereby creating a social network and developing a sense of social competence. They also have usually developed a secure attachment with one adult caregiver in infancy or have developed a relationship with one adult who has significant influence, such as a teacher. On the basis of a review of twenty-four studies of resilience Kimchi and Schaffner (1990) draw up a profile of the resilient adolescent. He or she is described as:

- well functioning;
- active;
- energetic;
- future orientated;
- achievement orientated;
- responsible;
- caring;
- nurturing;
- socially perceptive;
- socially mature;

and as having:

- positive self-concept;
- internal locus of control;
- belief in self-help;
- high internalised values.

Studies of family background factors in the development of resiliency indicate that caregivers reward and encourage risk-taking and independence and support the belief that personal effort will lead to success in the face of adversity, therefore stimulating internal locus of control (Werner 1989).

It is clear from the studies referred to so far that the social context is an important protective or risk factor. Family background factors, such as parenting style and parent–child relationships, influence the skills and attitudes of the young person. Other environmental influences, such as cultural style, socio-economic status and religious belief, have also been implicated (Felner *et al.* 1995). Pryor-Brown *et al.* (1986) found that children of unemployed parents experienced higher stress, demonstrated more socially inept behaviours and experienced greater peer rejection. Conger *et al.* (1994) identified that financial hardship within a family leads to more arguments and conflicts between the parents. These, in turn, contribute to higher levels of stress amongst the children. Although socio-economic disadvantage is correlated with greater stress, studies of competence and resilience have shown that, regardless of background, children are generally resourceful. Competence is the mediating variable that predicts positive or negative outcomes (Garmezy and Masten 1991).

Social support can be provided by the family, by peers or by other adults such as teachers. It is not only the actual availability of support that is protective but also the belief that others are available to provide emotional support. Compas *et al.* (1987) found a direct link between social support and psychological outcomes of stressful situations. Ryan (1989) investigated social support at different stages in stressful events in 103 8–12-year-olds. Ryan found that children used social support during a stressful experience, and avoidance and distracting strategies after a stressful experience. DuBois *et al.* (1992), however, compared levels of psychological distress following major events in students who had a high level of support from friends, family and school personnel with those in students who had a low level of support. In this study, students were followed up over a two-year period with measures of adaptation to major life events. They found no significant 'buffering effect' for friend or family support but did for support from school personnel. Although social support has been widely accepted as an important mechanism in successful management of stress, Gore and Colten (1991) point out some crucial gender differences. They note that adolescent girls' self-esteem is more dependent on relationships with others than boys' is. Furthermore, social support has greater importance than a sense of personal competency as a coping device for females. The opposite is true for males. Box 4.1 describes a particular instance of bullying between girls which illustrates some of these factors of support from school staff, and ways of dealing with pupils bullying others along lines recommended by whole-school policies.

The research into stress emphasises the importance of social support as both a protective factor and a coping strategy. Given that bullying is a social phenomenon and that increasing social support has been identified as an intervention strategy (Smith and Sharp 1994; Taylor 1996), it seems to be a key area for continuing study. Are there gender differences in the use and usefulness of social support in bullying situations? Does children's use of social support networks when they are being bullied vary from when they are experiencing other types of stressors? Has the success of social skills groups for bullied students arisen not only from skill development but also from the provision of a social support network through the group process itself?

Coping styles and strategies

Coping is another key element in the process of stress management. Coping can be defined as active efforts to resolve stress and to create reasonable solutions. How successfully or unsuccessfully we cope with stress will affect the extent and nature of the stress we experience. Hendren (1990) suggests that unsuccessful coping can, in the worst cases, lead to depression, suicide, substance abuse, eating disorders and other mental and physical illnesses.

Pearlin (1991) describes coping as having three functions:

- to change or adapt the circumstances giving rise to stress;
- to change the way we think and perceive the situation in ways which will minimise the potential for stress;
- to control and relieve the symptoms of distress which arise from the stressors.

Coping may address one particular function, not necessarily all three. Pearlin points out that some life difficulties can be very resistant to individual coping efforts. He suggests that this is particularly so when stressors are embedded in an organisation. In these circumstances, management of meaning and personal distress are more appropriate modes of coping than problem-solving. Sharp (1997) looked at coping strategies used by bullied students. She was expecting to find that pupils who were bullied less or who experienced less negative impact from bullying would use a different set of strategies from those pupils who were bullied more or who were more seriously affected by it. What she actually found was that the pupils who had experienced more bullying demonstrated greater versatility and resourcefulness in the range of coping strategies they employed. They were not reacting in a different way; rather it seemed that the strategies being used were ineffective in stopping the bullying. There may be a number of overlapping reasons why – possibly the behaviour of the children who were experiencing more bullying was slightly different in terms of intensity or persistence or some other non-verbal characteristic, from that of those who had experienced less, in spite of the children categorising their responses in the same way on the questionnaire survey. Alternatively, the effect of the victim's behaviour on the bully may have been different because of lack of support from an anti-bullying school culture. Certainly, the experience of school staff experienced in effective anti-bullying work is to stress the central importance of the whole-school, pupil-culture approach, and this is backed up by the research quoted in Chapter 6 of this book. Sharp (1997) took this latter approach, and she reflected on these results in the light of work on effective intervention against bullying which indicates that a whole-school or community approach is essential for achieving change. Consequently, she concluded that bullying should be perceived as an organisational stressor, in that it is persistent and resistant to individual action, requiring change at the group or organisational level.

Box 4.1 Case study: Anna and Helen – a tale of two girls at Ansfield High School

Anna joined the school halfway through the year when her family had to move after the sudden death of her father. She soon found her way around the school and started to go around with a few of the girls in her form. A few weeks later, after an argument, these girls turned on her and started to spread rumours that her father was not dead but had left the family suddenly. Other girls started teasing Anna about this and Anna became extremely upset. She tackled the girls about it, but this only made things worse, with the girls saying that she could not stand any jokes and was not good company for them. She tried to shrug it off, but that did not work either. Anna felt she had no one to turn to: she did not know any of the other girls well enough and she did not think that her form teacher would take the teasing seriously. She did not want to make her mother any more worried than she was already. She cried a lot at home, about the least of things, which was put down to delayed grief about her father's death. She had always been a very sociable girl, but now started to avoid going anywhere, even to clubs that she had enjoyed up to that time. She suffered from sleeplessness and lost weight. Eventually she refused to go to school and, when her mother took her to see her G.P., was diagnosed as depressed. Anna stayed away from school for at least six months until she was gradually reintroduced into school, with the help of a programme designed by the educational psychologist and work on peer support (see Chapter 6) carried out within the school.

   As a result of concern about bullying in the school, an anti-bullying policy was drawn up, involving all the stakeholders, including the pupils. About three months after this process had been started, Helen was attacked by a group of girls. The girls alleged that she had 'stolen' the boyfriend of one of them. They called her 'slag', pulled her hair and threw her to the ground. She was physically slightly hurt but was reluctant to go to her teacher about this, as she did believe that they may have had good reason to attack her. Her form teacher, however, noticed scratches on Helen's face and asked her about these. When Helen started to deny that anything was the matter, one of Helen's classmates, who had been a witness to the scene, fortunately intervened. This classmate was encouraged by the school's anti-bullying policy, which made it a duty for any pupil to tell when they knew of bullying taking place, so he decided to tell Helen's form teacher what the reasons were. The form teacher contacted the head of year and, as stated in the school's anti-bullying policy, saw all the girls involved in the bullying episode that same day, including the victim, the girls who bullied and the bystanders. Their discussion focused on what the group could do to avoid this recurring, how the perpetrators could make amends and how the bystanders could have helped the victim. The parents of the girls involved were also contacted to inform them of what had happened and try and gain their support. At the end of the session the girls apologised and are now able to work with each other without falling out.

- What systems should have been in place to prevent Anna's problem?
- How did the school's new anti-bullying policy help Helen?
- What factors were important in the rapid resolution of Helen's problem?

Summary and conclusions

There are various levels and intensities of bullying, and it is likely that the consequences are different for these different degrees of stress. This is likely to depend particularly on whether or not the attempts by the victims to avoid or resist the bullying are successful in the reasonably short term. Any bullying relationship which lasts for more than half a term will definitely have considerable negative emotional impact on the victim, as that length of time will mean that the early efforts to avoid or resist the unwelcome attentions will have failed. From there on, chronic and acute harm resulting from the stress will only increase. Some programmes can be directed to helping children become more resilient when facing this kind of stress, and these programmes will also be beneficial to children who are not at immediate risk from bullying. Implementing these kinds of curricular programmes in schools does need staff with interests and skills in teaching such programmes, and management who can protect the staff time and resources necessary for success.

Some questions to think about

- Many studies have concluded that poor self-esteem and self-confidence make children more likely to be victimised. How probable is it that these studies are reflecting the results of bullying rather than a predisposition to be chosen as a victim?
- Would being bullied during primary school years be likely to be more damaging than being bullied during adolescence?
- Do boys and girls use social support in the same way to protect themselves during periods of victimisation?
- Are the support mechanisms useful for victims of bullying also useful for protection from other forms of stress, for example family stress?
- Do social skills training groups for vulnerable children work as much by giving them experience of working with a supportive group as by giving them any transferable social skills?

Part II

Towards effective intervention

Chapter 5

Changing cultures

The story to date

As a result of current research into bullying we have a better understanding of what forms it takes and in which contexts it is most likely to happen. We know that it is a social phenomenon that relates to group behaviour, hierarchies and power relationships. We also know that levels of bullying are influenced by organisational factors. The research clearly suggests that one essential intervention is at the whole-school level (Olweus 1993; Smith and Sharp 1994; Roland 1998) and requires some investment of time and effort, actively involving most of the school community. This sets the cultural expectations and standards of behaviour that can support other more specific but essential interventions at the class and individual level. Sustaining change in levels of bullying has been problematic, as shown in various follow-up studies (Roland 1989b; Eslea and Smith 1994; Thompson 1995). Collectively, these studies suggest that bullying is highly resistant to change, except in organisations that consistently implement a systematic and high-profile organisational anti-bullying programme, lasting over a number of years, in a continuous review process. This programme runs alongside other pastoral programmes, such as behaviour policies and special needs policies. This anti-bullying programme must also include the specific procedures mentioned above at a class level, at the point of day-to-day dealing with bullying incidents with discipline in mind, and at a monitoring and review level. Effective monitoring and review leads to effective policy maintenance and success in keeping the levels of bullying down when the initial impact of the project has passed (see Box 5.1 which gives a history of one school's anti-bullying programme over a number of years).

Box 5.1 What happens when an anti-bullying policy is not maintained

Arora (1994) noted a substantial reduction, of approximately 20 per cent, in the extent of bullying taking place in a secondary school. This initial work took place over the two years 1986 to 1988. The senior management in this school had been intent to use a whole-school and community approach to reducing bullying during that period, with a number of specific innovations in pastoral procedures, and this clearly had positive effects. Nine years later, the school had had two changes of headteacher and an almost complete change of staff. The intake of the school had altered in terms of cultural background but had not changed otherwise. In 1997, a senior member of staff called in an educational psychologist as the school wished to have 'assistance with drawing up an anti-bullying policy'. When the level of bullying was measured in this school, using the same method as before (the Life in School checklist, see Appendix), the number of incidents reported by the pupils had increased, not only compared with the figures in 1988, but also compared with the level at which the school had started originally in 1986. What had happened in the intervening period was that, for various reasons, anti-bullying strategies had not been part of the school's development plan and were not therefore reviewed on a regular basis. The result was that the intensive and effective work carried out earlier had been forgotten, and the school had lost the benefits of the programme it had run successfully in the past.

Questions and concerns

Clearly, with the crucial need for the work to affect the whole school system, managers need to be as aware as possible of the implications of research from organisational psychology and educational management to implement and maintain such a programme of policies. This chapter explores some of the findings from that literature relevant to implementing anti-bullying programmes across the school, and goes on to consider some of the practical projects which may form part of a whole-school approach. The organisational and management literature is very broad, so this discussion can deal only with a highly selected extract from that research but one that is centrally relevant to these issues. Questions which will spring to mind when schools adopt anti-bullying policies are often quite simple, such as:

- How can I encourage colleagues to see bullying as an issue worthy of their energies and time?
- How many people will I need to form the core of a working group, and what responsibilities might they have in the school?
- Is it sensible to involve any outside consultants of any kind? If I do involve them, can I specify what I want them to do, and what should this be? Can I get such consultations free?
- Do we really have to consult the parents or children or governors?
- How much time will it take?
- How will anti-bullying policies relate to all the other policies we have – staff development, school development, staff induction, equal opportunities, pastoral policies, behaviour policies, special needs, parental involvement, anti-racist policies, curriculum policies, inclusion policies?
- How will the review processes for all these policies relate together?
- How much can managers delegate?
- Would involving staff with less managerial experience in the project group be a useful staff development experience for them?
- Can charismatic and very hardworking school leaders achieve an anti-bullying culture without bothering with these policies and consultations?

Key findings from the background research in organisational change

Sharp (1997) suggests that bullying should be conceptualised as an 'organisational stressor'. Organisational stressors (Pearlin 1991) are part of the very fabric of the organisation and are therefore particularly resistant to individual solutions, requiring change at the group or organisational levels. Defining bullying as an organisational stressor requires a shift in the way we think about bullying and the solutions to bullying behaviour we develop. Such a definition emphasises the social dynamics of bullying behaviour and acknowledges that multi-level group solutions will be more effective. Half-hearted, tokenistic or minimalist approaches will have limited or negligible impact.

This chapter considers the process of organisational change and then applies this to our understanding of establishing a whole-school approach.

The process of change

Lewin (1947) identified change as a three-stage process. The first stage ('unfreezing') involves helping people to identify and accept the reasons for change. This often involves people recognising that their current behaviour is ineffective or inappropriate, in effect creating dissatisfaction with things as they are. Once behaviours are 'unfrozen', then the second stage ('implementing change') can take place. There are many different ways in which change can be implemented. Strategies for change can usually be grouped into three categories (Chin and Benne 1976):

- strategies that emphasise the factual evidence base and rationale for change (empirical-rational);
- strategies that involve re-education and the agreement of new norms (normative-re-educative);
- strategies that coerce people to change (power-coercive).

Individuals vary in how they respond to the different kinds of change strategy, and successful change often involves employing strategies from across the three categories. For change to be sustained, the final stage of 'refreezing' has to occur, establishing and embedding the new behaviours and culture within the organisation. This is most effective when individuals internalise the change by adopting it as part of their self-image. 'Refreezing' is usually achieved by individuals trying out new behaviours within a positive and supportive environment, where their new behaviours are noticed and reinforced through praise and acknowledgement. Over time, this change is maintained through less frequent reinforcement.

Jacobs (1994) describes a formula for successful change attributed to David Gleicher. This is D×V×F>R:

Dissatisfaction × Vision × First Steps > Resistance to change.

Jacobs argues that all three factors D, V and F must be present. If any one of them is not present, then the impact of the other two, however strong, will be impaired and the resistance to change, which is ever-present within any organisation or group, will not be overcome. There are many reasons for resistance to change, some of which can help us to refine our proposed changes so they will be more effective. The following are the most important causes of resistance:

- lack of conviction that change is needed;
- dislike of imposed change;
- dislike of surprises;
- fear of the unknown;
- reluctance to deal with unpopular issues;
- fear of inadequacy or failure;
- disturbed practices, habits, routines and relations;
- lack of respect and trust in the person/people promoting change.

O'Connor (1993) classified resisters into four types: saboteurs, survivors, zombies and protesters. Saboteurs resist in a conscious but covert way: they may sow the seeds of dissent amongst colleagues but remain silent themselves. Survivors resist covertly but unconsciously: they may not be aware that any change is actually taking place. Zombies may agree with the changes but lack the will or the skills to implement them. Finally, protesters are overt and conscious in their resistance and consequently are the easiest to deal with. The various ways in which staff react to change have been described in a model developed by Rogers and Shoemaker (1971), who categorised staff into five groups, described as innovators, early adopters, early majority, late majority and laggards. The innovators and early adopters were seen as being quick to adapt to external change or new ideas, basing their approval on rational grounds of their understanding of the processes involved and early evaluations and trials of the changed procedures. In the research evidence considered, these were estimated to include about one-sixth of the typical organisational membership. The main group of staff, comprising about two-thirds of the whole group, formed the 'early majority' and 'late majority', who accepted change when they were convinced of its value by specific staff development, training, and by observing the evaluations of changed procedures. The 'late majority' were the more sceptical, tending to look for close-to-hand and personally relevant evaluation. The 'laggards', forming about one-sixth of the typical whole staff group, were seen by these researchers as being instinctively resistant to change and suspicious of new arrangements. For this group, rational arguments, empirical evaluations and even colleagues' views had little influence, and ultimately management had no option but to change the procedures round them and insist they changed their pattern of work.

This research is clearly putting forward a very general model, and the details will vary significantly between organisations, according to historical features of management patterns and success or failure in their local context. The model, however, does put forward, in a formal sense, the understanding many people have of the management of change – that individuals differ in their response to change, some behaving in a leading role in the adoption of new procedures and some being very reluctant to change, even when there is clear evidence of the relative success of the new procedures. It also emphasises that, to convince them of the desirability of change, different individuals require different types of evidence, some needing the rational and empirical, some needing the cultural confidence that 'everyone else is doing it', and some only responding to specific decisions by management and adoption of the new processes by the whole organisation.

All of the research on managing change suggests that resistance can be prevented and overcome through participation and involvement. This includes open discussion of individual resistance to change.

Whole-school anti-bullying approaches

There is a paucity of long-term, systematic evaluations of anti-bullying intervention programmes. Those that do exist (Thompson 1995; Roland and Munthe 1997; Eslea and Smith 1998) demonstrate that many schools, probably a majority, do not succeed in maintaining the reductions they achieved in levels of bullying behaviour over time periods of three to five years. Some schools, however, through a combination of consistent management and attention to maintenance of procedures from year to year, do manage to keep reducing the frequency of bullying over a three- to four-year period. What do we know from research of these processes?

Research studies into intervention strategies have demonstrated that levels of bullying can be reduced initially in most schools by the implementation of an agreed set of procedures for both prevention of and response to bullying behaviour. The procedures have to be implemented thoroughly and consistently throughout the school community (Olweus 1991; Smith and Sharp 1994). Staff, parents and carers, and pupils all have to be actively engaged in the process. It is this widespread community involvement in the process, backed up by specific procedures at class and individual level, which seems to be the critical factor in achieving significant shifts in levels of bullying behaviour.

The most effective interventions against bullying seem to be those which:

- involve the whole school community in discussing the problems and possible solutions;
- lead to clear understanding of what bullying is and what to do about it;
- result in consistent application of procedures for the prevention of bullying and response to particular incidents when they occur.

This can be achieved by developing a whole-school anti-bullying policy. A whole-school policy provides the framework for any type of intervention against bullying. Through the whole-school policy a school can make sure that everyone knows what they should do to prevent and respond to bullying. To increase the likelihood of the policy being successfully implemented, it should be based upon extensive consultation, with staff, students and parents, on policy principles and content about how people will treat each other in and around school. An emphasis should be placed on collective responsibility for tackling bullying. The implications of the policy for behaviour should be made clear, and staff, students and parents should be regularly reminded of this. When assessing how successful their policy is in practice, schools should avoid relying upon the 'feel-good' factor, as this can be deceptive. Data should routinely be collected, so that changes in student and staff behaviour and attitudes can be assessed.

Just having a policy is not enough to change behaviour within the school. It is quite easy for schools to have policies in place but not to have them fully effective. This is because of poor definition of aspects of the policies, which leads to individualistic interpretations of the policies and weak review processes. Effective school policies are those that are put into practice systematically and continuously.

A policy might contain:

- the aims of the school in relation to tackling bullying and promoting co-operative behaviour;
- a clear definition of behaviours which are considered to be bullying;
- details of preventative measures that will reduce the likelihood of people being violent towards each other, including a reward system for appropriate behaviour;

- strategies for encouraging students to tell a member of staff if they or a friend are experiencing bullying behaviour;
- definite guidelines for immediate and long-term action should bullying occur;
- definite guidelines for action should bullying or violence recur involving the same students;
- procedures for monitoring the success of the policy and for reviewing it, with indications of the group responsible for monitoring and review (e.g. governors or management team);
- implications of the policy for the behaviour of staff, students and parents.

Guidelines for action are also required for when there is a suspicion of bullying but no actual evidence. Bullying behaviour is rarely witnessed by adults and can be very difficult to prove, the teacher more often than not being faced with conflicting accounts of what has occurred. If unconfident about how to approach this kind of situation, the adult may choose a half-hearted response and leave the bullying behaviour unchallenged. Because there are usually more 'witnesses' who are part of the bullying group than there are victims, it is often very difficult to achieve clear, evidence-based identification of who are the culprits and what exactly happened. Even if the children do actually describe the same events, the meanings they give to the events are certain to be widely different. Some descriptions are given by the victims (hurt, frightened, and wanting to describe their experiences as injustices) and some by the bullies (confident, secure, and wanting to describe events as normal life). Nevertheless, the adult responsible will need to make some response in this grey area without being inconsistent with the school's behaviour policies. The Method of Shared Concern (Pikas 1989) and the No Blame Approach, based on similar assumptions (Maines and Robinson 1992), are both designed to deal with situations where there are conflicting accounts of events but one or more obvious victims. These are described in Chapter 7. A more general approach, based on group work with all concerned, including the parents, is described in Foster and Thompson (1991).

Process of establishing a whole-school approach

If a school wishes to either set up a new whole-school approach from scratch, or to have a general review of an existing policy where previously there has been no mechanism for review, the first action is to form a working group of about four to six people. This needs to have leadership from staff involved with the pastoral care system, a representative of the senior management team, and at least two people who feel a personal commitment to the issue and have a willingness to commit some time to the project. It also helps to have one or two semi-outsiders to provide accountability for the process. This could be a person acting in a consultant role from the LEA support staff, such as an educational psychologist with interests and knowledge in the area, a member of the behaviour support team with similar skills, or a parent or parent governor. Even if an outside consultant is not involved as a core member of the team, schools report it as helpful if such individuals are invited to some of the meetings of the group. It can also help in getting chunks of work done (such as analysing data) if one of the group members is doing a dissertation for a higher degree. This person has both a personal commitment to putting the time in to analyse the data and the support of an H.E. tutor to help along the processes of data analysis and interpretation.

Parental involvement

One crucial part of the whole process is the way parents are informed and involved, both in the consultations about the policy, and in the actual procedures used in school to challenge bullying. Contacts with parents can make school staff anxious, bringing them a feeling of slight unpredictability, and can be seen as opening doors to being pressurised in a vague and usually unproductive way. However, parents are almost always very supportive of anything schools can do to make life less aggressive for their children. They also understand quite a lot about the thin line between the necessary resisting of bullying, in their eyes usually by encouraging their children to stand up for themselves, and making the situation worse by provoking aggression from others (Trimingham 1994).

Many parents, however, have little knowledge of what 'learning to stand up for yourself' involves, apart from fighting back or involving a teacher. Many parents would also recognise the dangers in fighting back as a general guide, without reference to the context – they recognise the dangers of escalation. At this point, the parents have a need to understand how the school is trying to minimise bullying, so that their advice to their children has some relationship to what staff in school are saying. Even if parents have sympathetic approaches to the pupils who are victims, and even to those who are doing the bullying, these sympathetic attitudes by themselves do not automatically translate into appropriate behaviour for their own children (Eslea 1997).

School staff are aware of the need to tell parents what they are doing in the anti-bullying policy and how the policy is not a reaction to what may be seen as a special problem for their particular school, but is a reasonable response to the DfEE's expectation that every school should have an effective anti-bullying policy in place which is reviewed at regular intervals (DfEE 1994, 2000). Parental approval of the school's efforts is almost universal in the UK, the usual critique being that the school could and should do more to combat bullying. Schools like parental approval of their efforts but, at the same time, are often wary of apparently encouraging parents to complain about bullying at school when it is exceedingly difficult for schools to stop all victimisation. How can schools set up a means for parents to take a realistic role in the anti-bullying programme, a role which recognises their concerns but does not give them unrealistic expectations of the school's success?

The basic principles behind parental involvement can be summarised as encouraging parents to understand that the school's policies are based on:

- stating the values of a safe and relaxed school atmosphere where children can learn effectively, and emphasising that aggression and violence in school is generally unacceptable, particularly where it takes the form of bullying
- identifying children who bully, and preventing them from continuing to do so
- identifying and supporting children who may be vulnerable to being isolated and victimised
- expecting parents to participate in direct anti-bullying work if their own children are involved in bullying, either as pupils who bully or as victims (Besag 1989)
- expecting parents to help their own children to develop social skills and confidence, by encouraging their children to express their own needs appropriately without hurting others with whom they come into contact. Social learning such as this, is just as relevant at home as it is at school (Randal 1996)

• expecting parents to make efforts to encourage communication with their children, by letting children talk about what they want to talk about and making space to listen to them. Many parents fall into the trap of assuming that the way to get children to talk is to ask them questions. However, by doing this, the adult maintains control of the agenda for communication and invites rejection of the topic by the child (Wood *et al.* 1986). Few adults would say more than a couple of sentences about topics in which they had no interest and no desire to tell anyone about. Listening when the child wants to talk about uncertainties or worries, even if they are very slight by adult standards, is crucial in preparing the way for students to feel they can talk to their parents about rejection and being bullied.

This last point is very important, as there is a little research evidence that when adolescents are asked: 'If you were being bullied, would you tell your parents?', a large majority of them say: 'No' (Thompson and Arora 1991). When asked to elaborate, the two most common reasons given were either that they believed their parents 'wouldn't want to know', or that, in the child's view, their parents would over-react by immediately taking control of the agenda out of the pupil's hands and rushing to school to confront the teaching staff.

Specifically, at what points in the school routines can parents become involved? The assertive ones will quickly become involved when invited – the question is how can the average parent be contacted effectively? There are various points of contact: the initial visit to school before admission, through detailed comment in the prospectus and circulation of the actual policy to new parents along with other details about school, through parental meetings relating to the operation of the parent governor system, and through explicit consultation about possible developments of the policy when the policy is reviewed. Each school will work out its own pattern of involvement, or a pattern will emerge by default. The pattern one school reached is outlined in the case study in Box 5.2.

Help from outside consultants

Ideally, good local contacts between schools and parents, and an active anti-bullying policy involving the students, should reduce the need to contact any of the national charitable organisations with interests in supporting parents and children in bullying situations,

Box 5.2 Case study: involving parents in the implementation of the anti-bullying policy

At Petersfield High School (a comprehensive school, in a mixed housing area, on the edge of an industrial town in the north of England), the initial impetus for setting up the anti-bullying policy had come from parent representatives on the school Welfare Committee asking questions about the extent of bullying in the school. A survey conducted with the help of the local educational psychology service had demonstrated that the children thought there was more bullying than the teachers had expected, and the Welfare Committee recommended that ways of reducing the bullying should be discussed with groups of adults and students across the school and a project committee, consisting largely of staff, should be set up to manage the process. The headteacher was very supportive of this initiative, as she felt it fitted in well with one of the general strategic aims of the senior management team – to reduce the level of aggression expressed between the students in the school and improve their behaviour towards each other.

As parents were involved in the initial setting up of the policy and its procedures, the project committee felt that parents should continue to be involved in the implementation of the policy as far as possible. School staff recognised that parents could be helpful in dealing with unacceptable behaviour from the students generally, and good communication between the staff and the parents about bullying incidents was considered to be helpful in dealing with these incidents. In addition, when pupils did complain to their parents that they were being bullied, parents usually complained to the school, some loudly and persistently, that the staff were not doing enough to stop the bullying. The project team felt that recognising parents' concerns before any incidents happened, and having strategies in place and well understood, went some way to easing parents' initial concern and demonstrated to them, when they were complaining of actual bullying incidents, that the school did take the issues seriously.

The policy, as finally agreed by the school community after consultations, did include recognition that there was a contract between the school and the parents as regards recognising and dealing with bullying. The parents' main roles were:

• to spend time with their children and try to encourage them to talk about their life in school, including the difficult areas;

- to come and discuss their concerns with school if they thought their children were having difficulties due to bullying – absolute proof was not required that the reasons for the child's difficulties were bullying;
- to join in with the school's procedures, as requested by the school, if their child was involved in bullying incidents, as either victim, bully, or supporter of the victim or the principal student doing the bullying;
- to try to attend the various, but infrequent, meetings arranged by school to keep in touch with parents, such as Parent–Teacher Association meetings or parents evenings of various types, when, from time to time, parent representatives on the various managing or advisory committees would be reporting back on the evaluations of the anti-bullying policy.

New parents were informed of the anti-bullying policy and various other areas of concern to the school – attendance, other aspects of the behaviour and discipline policies, uniform, how the school was organised into year groups and classes – at a special parents evening for new parents in the July before their child joined the school. In order to give the greatest opportunity for discussion so that parents could express their views and ask questions, the meeting was organised as a number of discussion groups, with six or eight parents to one member of school teaching staff per group. If any supplementary staff, such as probationary teachers or members of the school's support staff from the LEA were available, they joined in with the discussion groups, as extra school staff. The discussion was organised to encourage parents to talk about their concerns and hopes for their children, prompted by a number of discussion cards for each group. The cards described a number of typical situations which parents might encounter as their children progressed through the school, such as a pupil wanting to walk to school rather than go on the school bus, or wanting to come home at lunchtime even though the journey was too long. Only some of the discussion cards referred to bullying – other matters were also included, as indicated above. Organising the meeting in this way meant that parents were able to think through for themselves the implications of the various matters the school wished them to consider, and they were able to feel that they could communicate with at least one member of the school staff. They were also able to meet other parents whom they might encounter in the future, and realised that their particular concerns were shared by other parents and often, indeed, by the staff as well. The senior management team's contribution was limited to introducing the meeting, saying a very few words about the various ways in which parents could contribute to the life of the school, and emphasising the importance of parents and teachers communicating with each other, so that the students gained the most from their school years.

These evenings did need some preparation, as can be imagined. All the staff needed to be familiar with the issues raised by the method and the discussion cards, and the less-experienced ones needed some practice in allowing parents to express their concerns and treat them as real, rather than immediately giving a prepared answer designed to close the discussion. All staff were expected to attend, even if they did not teach the first year, so that there were enough staff for each group of parents to have at least one staff member to chair the discussion, and so that the less-experienced members could join in a group with a more-experienced teacher. This training took up most of the staff meeting preceding the parents evening and was, in fact, a good opportunity for the staff to come together to clarify their views and reach a consensus on what the school's position was on some of the issues.

This particular school's governors had agreed that the person responsible for initiating the process of evaluating and reviewing the working of the anti-bullying policy was one of the parent-governors, and that this process should occur not less than once every two years, using a variety of information, including some survey data collected by the students. The role of the parent-governor also included reporting back to parent meetings what the evaluation had demonstrated. The parent-governor was included as a member of the anti-bullying project group and so had access to the experiences of the teaching staff to guide the review process. In this way, parental interests were central to the whole policy, and the school had access to an extra source of energy and activity to help drive the anti-bullying process.

such as Kidscape, Childline (MacLeod and Morris 1996) or the NSPCC. However, it would help discussion inside school if some of their materials were available for the staff to illustrate the resources available outside the school gates and the strength of the concern driving these organisations. Staff may well decide to use some of this material in their establishment of the policy in school.

If the school wishes to set up a specific contract with an outside consultant, then the core tasks for which the consultant is needed (i.e., the tasks most in-school groups find it hardest to do effectively by themselves, as they have least overlap with the usual school activities and need extra committal of time to complete) are:

- establishing the process of data analysis from the initial incidence survey;
- establishing the balance of anti-bullying activities across all levels in school – the whole-school level, the class level, and the individual level;
- identifying training needs for the staff concerned;
- identifying the relationship between anti-bullying policies and other pastoral policies – normally, that all policies should include reference to each other, should indicate which policy has precedence in particular situations, and should not be contradictory in detail (Thompson and Sharp 1994);
- identifying monitoring data that ought to be collected and review processes;
- design of induction processes for new staff. One of the major reasons why anti-bullying processes decay in many schools is the lack of any induction training for new staff, including senior staff and new headteachers. Schools do have periods of rapid staff turnover and may easily lose staff with experience of how the anti-bullying project works.

Planning to avoid policy decay

What are the reasons for policy decay? Thompson (1995) reports on a follow-up study of secondary schools two years after the end of an anti-bullying intervention that had produced a significant reduction in bullying. This showed that in schools where there was now more bullying taking place than there had been two years ago, the staff and the children were perfectly well aware that the school was putting less effort into the anti-bullying work than it had done previously. The staff saw this as being because:

- The original anti-bullying project leader had left the school, usually for promotion, or had changed position inside the school, and no one else had taken over the role.
- New members of the senior management team had been appointed from outside the school, and they had different priorities for school development. This could be particularly damaging to the health of the anti-bullying policy when the

new member of staff was the head, with prior commitment to alternative school developments. This was seen to run counter to the approach of a whole-school policy, where realistic consultation with others, including the children, was crucial for effectiveness.

- There was little or no effective induction for new staff or new cohorts of children into the anti-bullying policy and its expectations and procedures. Induction in the pastoral, disciplinary and anti-bullying procedures is clearly crucial for the effective integration of new staff into school routines. New groups of pupils need a complete re-run of the original project which established the policy in the school, including the philosophy of the project, the current operation of the policy, and enough group work to give them a feeling of involvement in and ownership of the process. Older groups need a restatement of the aims and processes of the policy and the chance to comment and suggest ways of improving it. This has to be done in a way which is not a straight repeat of the original experience, but includes enough new material, still related to the topic, to represent a development of this particular part of the pastoral curriculum. If such new material is not included and the presentation of the refresher course is the same as the initial work the year previously, both staff and children will feel (and are likely to say) that they 'did' bullying last year, and pay minimal attention. Such refresher courses can often be included in discussions related to the mainstream curriculum topics, as well as in the Personal, Social and Health Education (PSE) curriculum.
- New DfEE and central government initiatives were taken up with all-consuming energy, leaving no one having any time for maintaining even the clearly successful earlier policies and procedures.
- The policy was never reviewed in a formal sense. This may have been a symptom, rather than a cause, of incipient neglect but the result was that there was never a point in time when influential staff discussed the policy, how effective it was, and what needed changing. Related to this, there was no on-going consultation with the students and other groups of people in school on the necessary policy changes.
- The policy did not specify what data should be collected, and when, to help with the policy reviews whenever they took place. The lack of a review date or a responsible body or person to

carry out the review also meant there was never any incentive to gather data to assess the effectiveness of the policy, as there was never any assurance or expectation that it would ever be used.

Conclusions

Many of the developments and changes in schools happen in response to pressure of events, and the above list of reasons given for policy decay illustrates well how events build up to cause real change in aspects of organisational operations. Some appreciation of these factors at the beginning of the policy development process can lead to some defensive action against decay being included from the outset. The following chapter considers some of the details of the agendas and tasks for the anti-bullying project group.

Some questions to think about

- Should anti-bullying programmes always have a high priority in school?
- Should parent-governors be given the role of initiating reviews of the effectiveness of the anti-bullying work?
- Should all the 'welfare policies' (anti-bullying, behaviour, anti-racist, etc.) be reviewed together in school, or kept apart?
- Would effective anti-bullying policies have any relationship to pupil achievement?
- How can school managers promote anti-bullying programmes without giving the impression that their school has a particular problem?

Chapter 6

Managing the anti-bullying project in school

'Unfreezing' and creating dissatisfaction with the current situation

In practice, one of the most uncertain stages in the development of whole-school anti-bullying policies is the initial phase, when the school management or a newly constituted project team has the challenge of persuading colleagues to give the issues some priority amongst the flow of events in school. The organisational theories referred to earlier can give some guidance.

Motivation to change is most easily achieved through the presentation of data about actual levels of bullying in the school, which are usually far greater than teachers expect, alongside information about the impact of bullying on individuals. The former can be collected via a whole-school survey, and the latter is available from research studies (see Chapter 4) and from media coverage of individual cases. Presenting data about the level of bullying within the school itself reduces the likelihood of 'discounting'. Discounting is a common reaction to possible change, whereby a person ignores or minimises aspects of the situation. In relation to bullying this may be manifested by staff, parents and pupils saying things like: 'We don't have a problem here,' or 'It's only a problem for a small minority of pupils.' It is easy for people to discount data which have been collected in another school, but data collected within their own school are more likely to convince people that there is a problem with bullying. For some staff, parents and pupils, the fact that there is bullying going on will be sufficient to convince them that action should be taken, but other people may discount the impact of bullying behaviour. For these individuals, factual data and vivid illustrations of the impact of bullying are required to motivate action.

An example of a dramatic approach to increasing understanding of the impact of bullying can be found in Finland. Bjørkqvist and Osterman (1999) describe the work of Timo Nuutinen, who collected together a set of photographs and X-ray slides showing the real-life injuries of bullied pupils. He toured schools in Finland with his shocking slide-show, each picture accompanied by a verbal account of how the injuries occurred. Bjørkqvist and Osterman evaluated the impact of Nuutinen's slide-show and lecture by measuring pupil attitudes towards bullying at three points in time: before the presentation, four days after and, finally, five months after. They found that amongst their sample of 12 to 16-year-olds, there was a short-term increase in pupils' disapproval of bullying and long-term impact on their awareness of the dangers of violent acts.

Establishing a vision of the future and realistic, achievable first steps

The development of an action plan must quickly follow the awareness-raising phase. Indeed, in the Sheffield anti-bullying programme these elements were combined in a staff development programme which included the presentation and discussion of the results of the school's own bullying survey, and presentation of data and illustrative accounts of the short- and long-term impact of bullying (including reference to well-publicised incidents nationally where pupils had been seriously injured or had died). The programme then went on to a discussion of options for intervention and agreement about which strategies the staff would implement. Typically, all staff (including non-teaching staff) and governors would be included in this training programme, and it would be followed by similar events for pupils and parents/families. In effect, what was established here was a 'whole-system event' leading to 'transformational change'. Businesses, faced with the need to change radically and quickly in order to continue to compete in the marketplace, have developed various processes for achieving significant cultural and behavioural change. A particular methodology has developed, sometimes called 'real-time change' or 'whole-system change', which involves bringing all the people within a community together to develop a new way of working or new plan for the future. Although the logistics can sometimes be mind-blowing, sometimes involving more than 2,000 people in different types of activity round the same theme, the level of engagement and participation prevents and overcomes resistance and results in more significant and far-reaching change. It was evident that within the schools in the Sheffield anti-bullying project, such whole-school events which included representatives from other groups were followed by notable reductions in bullying behaviour. This supports the theory that cultural transformation and behaviour change across an organisation are most easily achieved via a whole-system event which takes people through the necessary processes of identifying reasons to change, establishing a vision for the future and agreeing realistic first steps.

Each school in the Sheffield project also established a small working 'project group', drawing on different community stakeholder groups – pupils, staff, parents, governors and representatives from local agencies such as police. This small group included the 'innovators' and 'early adopters' within the school staff and, as such, established an energetic and enthusiastic force for co-ordinating the implementation of the agreed action. At times when energy might be flagging within the general population or when attention was directed elsewhere, this group would provide an internal reminder and reinforcer of the change process. Parents can give welcome impetus to the project group at this stage and, in general, their support is very well worth seeking out and encouraging (Eslea 1997; Eslea and Smith 2000).

Establishing the anti-bullying programme – the tasks for the project group

There are a number of specific tasks for the project group to achieve, which will result in a controlled unfolding of the whole anti-bullying programme. Many of these have been referred to in other chapters and in other sections of this chapter, but here they are all drawn together. If an active anti-bullying programme is already in place from previous years, then many of these tasks will have been thought about and procedures devised already. If this is the case, then the tasks are that much easier and quicker to achieve, as they contain a major element of review and possible amendment of decisions, followed by implementation.

- Decide on the ideal membership of the group and the pattern of relationships and communication with the senior management team, governors, parents, the bulk of the teaching staff, the non-teaching staff and students. The stage of setting up the group needs the support of the senior management team and possibly one of them as a member. The pattern of communications between the group and the rest of the school is the core statement of the 'whole-school' characteristics of the policy and the resulting programme. Communication is usually through agenda items and documents to other committees or working groups, supported by a presentation by someone from the project group. Occasionally, circular letters to other large groups are necessary.

- Discuss and decide on the best ways of gathering some quantifiable data about the extent of bullying and whether the school needs any external support in doing this. Existing published materials in the research and commercial literature can give a good start in this, and imaginative teaching projects in the pastoral or curriculum areas can provide much more localised information. Chapter 3 gives a detailed discussion of this phase of activity.

- Implement the surveys, including ways of scoring the results (students can help) and feeding the results back to the staff and other stakeholders, in a digestable form. The group needs to take responsibility here for deciding on a form of presentation to the various groups that makes sense to them. When the surveys are done for the first time, the results usually show higher levels of bullying or bullying behaviour than anybody expects, and this in itself gives an impetus to the project.

- Set up consultation activities with the various groups (including, in particular, parents and students) on matters which need reviewing in the existing policy or which should be included in a new policy. Consultation exercises with students are particularly useful, as they are well aware of the detailed circumstances in which bullying occurs in school.

- Collect the results of the consultations, and amend the existing policy or write the new one. In both cases, the document should be seen as a draft to be circulated to the various stakeholders, asking for their comments. This detailed consultation should not be seen only as seeking views – it also works as a dissemination activity, strengthening the understanding and knowledge of the whole-school community about the school's position on bullying.

- Following final review, disseminate the policy document to the groups of stakeholders.

- Discuss and decide on what specific interventions are needed and relevant in school to give specific and local focus to the anti-bullying activities. At this point, the best advice is to initiate two or three interventions well rather than to attempt more, as there is usually a dearth of staff with training in non-curricular interventions. Often, external groups can help at this stage, particularly LEA support services, either with planning or by providing extra pairs of hands for specific projects. One type of intervention that is often necessary, usually involving pastoral staff and usually based on the 'methods of common concern', is one to deal specifically with students suspected of bullying others. This intervention is important because otherwise the only way of addressing students who bully others is under the general disciplinary procedures, when there is clear 'evidence' that they are indeed the ones involved. Due to the hidden nature of bullying and its tendency to occur within groups of children who support the bullying students, such 'evidence' is very difficult to collect and, if nothing happens, the victim's pessimism that nothing can be done is vindicated. The alternative approaches illustrated in the next chapter, which are specifically designed to deal with situations where there is no clear 'proof' of which individual is doing the bullying, or where many individuals are partially involved, are much more satisfactory for use in these circumstances.

• Complete a training audit of the training needs of the school staff, to lay a firm foundation for the anti-bullying programme. This may involve group-work skills for staff involved with the pastoral programme, counselling skills for those involved with interventions to support victims of bullying and other vulnerable students, and specific project training for those implementing the other interventions. This stage needs liaison with the staff development group.

• Set up monitoring and review methods: which surveys should be repeated and when, which groups should be involved in the analysis, and when should the effectiveness of the programme be reviewed? In practice, this is likely to be at yearly intervals. Review periods longer than one year apart run the risk of momentum being lost. To which groups should the results of the review be reported? How should the results be made known to the school generally? It is tempting to want to keep relative failure quiet by avoiding publicity, but this also has the effect of avoiding the re-launch of the programme and sets the scene for the gradual decline in the effectiveness of the anti-bullying work.

• Set up a timetable for the dissemination of the policy to the new group of students joining the school in September, and induction programmes for new staff.

The project group does need to be a standing group from one year to the next, and it does need to continue to receive the support of the senior management team over time. As members leave due to the usual career changes, they need to be replaced and the work they do does need to be valued by the school leaders. In practice, members of the anti-bullying group often find it is a good base for developing their teaching career, and the current school leaders often find the project group to be a good training ground for the next generation of middle-managers in school.

The procedures in junior schools are somewhat simpler than in secondary schools, as there are fewer people to become involved, but the principles remain the same. The case studies in Boxes 6.2 and 6.3 on pp. 121 and 124 give a detailed picture of how two schools – one a high school and one a junior school – progressed to a complete programme plan.

'Refreezing' and maintaining change

Roland and Munthe (1997) discuss the process of change in the schools involved in the Norwegian study. Roland followed up the progress of forty schools in the Norwegian county of Rogaland three years after a national campaign had begun to establish an anti-bullying programme across all of Norway. In Rogaland, by the end of the initial intervention programme, the level of bullying in the schools had been reduced significantly. At the three-year follow-up point, however, Roland found that overall, average levels of bullying across all the schools were slightly higher than the level before the intervention had started. In other words, the effects of the intervention had washed out after a three-year period. This was in marked contrast to the results of a follow-up done one and two years after the initial campaign in forty schools in Bergen, a neighbouring county to Rogaland, where levels of bullying had initially fallen on average by 50 per cent. On analysing the data from Rogaland more closely, Roland established that some schools, where there was a high level of support from the headteacher and where the principles and programmes had been implemented thoroughly and consistently, had maintained sizeable reductions in the levels of bullying.

However, he noticed the beginnings of a trend for schools to revert to 'normal' once the impetus of the national campaign lessened. It was almost as if the impact of the national campaign had been lost as soon as it finished. He noted also the benefits of outside assistance, in the form of support from educational psychologists, specialist teachers and advisers. Schools which were visited, albeit infrequently, by an interested and knowledgeable person were more likely to achieve and sustain change. He also considered ways in which the programme itself may have contributed to its unsustainability in most schools. He recognised that schools experience a wide array of problems and concerns related to maintaining discipline and constructive relationships, of which bullying is only one. How realistic and practical is it to expect schools to maintain an emphasis on bullying? Would it not be more effective to find ways in which schools could tackle bullying as part of a wider approach to maintaining discipline and promoting co-operative behaviour? Roland concluded that to achieve long-term change, the following factors were required:

- class-based programmes aimed at tackling other behavioural problems as well as bullying;
- methods to illustrate and discuss bullying with each class;
- a specific intervention strategy to stop bullying;
- a whole-school action plan which integrates the above and which involves staff, parents/carers and pupils;
- organised, professional assistance from outside the school;
- a system of support from the Ministry of Education and from LEAs.

Roland went on to research these contentions, specifically the first, as he felt this was a crucial element in the success of the programmes. He demonstrated that by setting up training programmes for experienced staff in classroom management, including behaviour management, he could demonstrate outcomes whereby the levels of bullying fell as well as other forms of anti-social behaviour (Roland 1998). The second Norwegian campaign against bullying has incorporated all of these elements, and early indicators suggest it is successful.

Both clear commitment from school leadership and assistance from outside the school are likely to encourage 'refreezing' in the new patterns of behaviour. If the headteacher shows obvious interest in the implementation of the anti-bullying approach then his or her comments on staff behaviour will serve to reinforce and encourage adoption of new ways of working. The involvement of the national government will also reinforce the importance of implementing anti-bullying strategies and may even serve to coerce unwilling staff to change. Visits from an interested and knowledgeable outsider will provide intermittent reinforcement and remind people of the importance of change. This might be combined with repeated surveys of levels of bullying, to provide evidence of the effectiveness of change, and the setting of annual targets to address specific aspects of bullying within the school. (For a specific example, see Box 6.3 on p. 124.)

National government interest and involvement

The involvement and interest of national government in anti-bullying initiatives can often be vital elements in stirring schools into action. Government interest is often followed by changes in legislation and guidance and/or funding to support new initiatives. National government involvement was a feature of both Norwegian anti-bullying campaigns, as it was in Scotland in the late 1980s and in England, Wales and Northern Ireland in the early 1990s. Government interest provides legitimacy and a sense of priority to the issue. Certainly, government interest in the UK has shifted bullying from a concern of parents and carers that was dealt with on an individual, case-by-case basis in a low-key manner to a high-priority matter for whole-school attention. One of the most important changes to have occurred is to alter definitions of a 'good' school. In the early to mid-1980s, the view that 'good schools don't have bullying' was prevalent. By the mid-1990s this had changed to: 'all schools have some bullying – good schools take action against it.'

The motivation for tackling bullying at a national level often stems from either a personal interest from ministers and/or as a result of strong lobbying from parental groups. Unfortunately, it is often the tragic death or severe injury of a child that acts as the catalyst for action at this level. This has been the case in Scandinavia, Japan and the UK.

The typical pattern for involvement is first to fund research into the nature and extent of bullying behaviour in schools. This is then followed by provision of an information pack for schools, guiding them in appropriate action. In the UK, the Department for Education and Employment (DfEE) followed up its information pack ('Don't suffer in silence') with funding for schools and LEAs to support training initiatives and whole-school development. Although it did not make it mandatory for schools to have an anti-bullying policy at that stage, it introduced the requirement for evidence of the schools' anti-bullying policy in practice as part of the regular inspections of schools. In 1998, as part of the new Schools Standards and Frameworks Act, this was strengthened further by requiring schools to establish a policy against bullying and to disseminate this annually to parents, pupils and staff. The DfEE have updated their original pack of information, so a new edition of 'Don't suffer in silence' is currently available to schools.

Local Education Authority interest and involvement

On matters of key importance, LEAs provide guidance, advice and training to schools. LEAs often follow government interest with local initiatives. Parents and carers who are concerned about their child being bullied will commonly complain to the LEA or their local councillor if they feel that the problem is not being taken seriously or tackled appropriately by the school. Over the last few years, there has also been an increase in the number of parents willing to take legal action against the school and LEA where bullying has continued unresolved for a period of time.

Typical LEA action might include provision of a local anti-bullying policy and guidance to schools, conferences and training events, and opportunities for schools to work closely with psychologists, education social workers or behaviour-support teachers to develop their practice and policies. Box 6.1 illustrates how one LEA provides support for schools in its area, and the final part of this chapter illustrates how another LEA has attempted to support its schools to maintain the quality of its anti-bullying programmes over time.

The benefits of local and national interest in providing impetus for change was documented by Roland (1998) and has been commented on elsewhere in this chapter. It seems that the interested outsider has a vital role to play in supporting the change process within schools.

Box 6.1 Birmingham LEA's anti-bullying campaign

This is the second anti-bullying campaign the LEA has mounted, the first being in the early 1990s. The campaign is aimed at the whole community, including schools, and combines awareness-raising and direct support to schools that wish to review and revamp their policies and practices. Key elements of the campaign include the following:

- Every letter sent out to schools from the Education Service contains a fact about bullying – for example:
  - One in four primary-aged pupils and one in ten secondary-aged pupils are bullied each term.
  - One in twenty pupils is bullied relentlessly day in, day out. Often this lasts for months and even years. Who are these pupils in your school?
  - One in three pupils feels ill and has difficulty concentrating when he or she is bullied. Improve pupil achievement by tackling bullying.
  - 5 per cent of pupils take time off school to avoid being bullied. Improve attendance by tackling bullying.
  - Whole-school approaches that actively involve all governors, staff, pupils and as many parents/carers as possible are the most effective in reducing bullying. Join our anti-bullying campaign to find out more.

- A series of posters has been designed to emphasise core messages in the campaign. These are being sent to each school and are being displayed on advertising boards around the city at three different times during the year.
- Local press coverage (radio and newspaper) has announced the campaign and reiterated key messages.
- The NSPCC has produced a leaflet for children and young people that has been distributed to all schools.
- A pamphlet on how to tackle bullying will be sent to each school.
- There will be a 'launch week' of training events for school staff, governors, parents/carers, pupils, and staff in health, social services and police authorities.
- A team of psychologists, behaviour-support teachers and educational welfare officers will work with individual schools that wish to review/develop their policy and practice.

A local authority initiative to reduce bullying: the Derbyshire Anti-bullying Commitment (ABC) Quality Assurance Scheme

Sometimes local authorities can intervene to assist schools in setting up their anti-bullying schemes or maintaining them over time. In Derbyshire, joint action between parents and local authority officers led to the setting up of an LEA scheme to recognise and support schools that had implemented effective anti-bullying programmes.

Background

During 1995, a small group of parents in Derby approached the LEA to discuss their concerns about bullying in schools. One of the outcomes of these discussions was the development of a framework for an accreditation scheme by Derbyshire's Anti-Bullying Course and Conference Group and the Anti-Bullying Consultation Group. The LEA then seconded two teachers from its schools to the Advisory and Inspection Service to help set up the scheme. They were assisted in this by seventeen development schools and by colleagues from the different education support services, who formed the County Accreditation Team. Over a period of three years, more than thirty schools joined the scheme. In 1998 there was a break in the funding, but the scheme is now active again, with over a hundred schools in the area showing an interest. At present, there are fourteen people in the County Accreditation Team (educational psychologists, education social workers, behaviour-support teachers and some headteachers). These people are responsible not only for the accreditation but also for the training and support of the schools taking part. Derbyshire LEA funds the scheme, but applications for sponsorship will be made in order to help expand the scheme (Priest 2001).

Aims of the scheme

The principal objective is to recognise, maintain and celebrate the work of teachers and schools in both preventing and dealing with bullying. In order to achieve this, the following is provided:

• a clear and effective framework on which to base a range of anti-bullying policies;

- recognition (through accreditation) of schools that have success-fully reached different stages in the process of setting up anti-bullying policies;
- support and training for schools while they are developing anti-bullying policies;
- encouragement to schools to go through a regular cycle of review and maintenance of their anti-bullying policies.

Outline and process of the framework for accreditation

Schools who join the scheme work towards the achievement of a Certificate of Commitment, followed by a series of awards:

- Initial Award of Good Practice;
- Interim Award of Good Practice;
- Award of Excellence.

The awards are based on the school's work in five key areas of intervention and prevention:

- staff development;
- curriculum;
- ethos;
- procedures and communication;
- monitoring, evaluation and research.

Each area has a number of different targets ('indicators'), which are graded according to levels of importance for good practice. The awards are based on the school's achievement of a number of these indicators. Each award denotes a more extensive range of anti-bullying measures.

Schools are also provided with a pack that gives ideas for anti-bullying strategies, and there is training available for the co-ordinator and other staff.

In order to register for the scheme, the school identifies a co-ordinator, who sets up a small quality assurance team and, if he or she so wishes, a larger working group. The co-ordinator oversees an initial audit of the school's anti-bullying policy, which is based on the scheme's indicators. After a baseline assessment, an action plan is drawn up which shows the indicators the school will work towards to achieve the first of the three awards. The evidence of action in this registration phase is put together in a portfolio, together with the action plan. When this is approved, the school will receive a Certificate of Commitment.

The co-ordinator, with the help of the quality assurance team and the working group, works towards achieving the indicators for the next award. Once the indicators have been achieved, the portfolio of evidence, together with an action plan for reaching the next award, is presented for accreditation to an accreditation panel. In Derbyshire, the school and LEA officers carry out accreditation, but in another LEA which is developing the scheme at the moment, peer accreditation may be introduced.

The Director of Education usually gives out the awards at a special ceremony. After the school has achieved the three awards, an Annual Review Certificate is obtained for evidence of the maintenance and extension of anti-bullying work.

Schemes of this type should give effective support to schools aiming to maintain the effectiveness of their policies.

Understanding the pace of change

Although the major research projects exploring the impact of whole-school interventions suggest that substantial reductions in levels of bullying may be observable within the first year, this is not always the case. In the DfEE-funded Sheffield anti-bullying project, the research team found that the effect of the whole-school policy was different in primary schools to secondary schools. In primary schools, there was an almost immediate effect on the levels of reported bullying. Some schools saw decreases of up to 80 per cent. In schools that had done little to tackle the problem, bullying had stayed the same or had increased. In secondary schools, reductions in levels of reported bullying decreased less dramatically, with little change at all in some cases. There was, however, a very marked increase of the number of students who would tell a teacher if they were being bullied and a similar increase in the number of students who would help someone who was being bullied. Two years later, in a follow-up study (Thompson 1995), those secondary schools which had continued to implement the policy actively with the original level of commitment had achieved continued reductions in levels of bullying and had continued to increase the supportive attitude of the students. However, these schools were only a minority of those which took part in the project, although all of them had initially volunteered to join.

In practical terms, the schools in the DfEE anti-bullying project took on average three terms to establish their whole-school anti-bullying approaches. Fonzi *et al.* (1999) describe a three-year process within one middle school. In the first year, the focus of intervention was the teaching staff, teaching them to manage psychosocial risk factors in schools. In the second year, the emphasis widened to include parents, raising awareness about the problem of bullying. A counselling service was provided for teachers to support them in tackling bullying behaviour. In the third year, the whole school community was involved with the intervention, through the development of a whole-school policy and also through curriculum programmes on tackling bullying. Evaluation of this programme indicated a marked effect on levels of bullying and an improvement generally in social relationships amongst peers.

Box 6.2 Case study: drawing up a whole-school anti-bullying policy at Ansfield High School

Awareness-raising

Some of the staff at Ansfield High School had become concerned at the number of bullying incidents that were being reported by parents, dinner supervisors and, occasionally, pupils themselves. One of the year heads agreed to do a survey amongst the pupils to see whether there was indeed a high incidence.

Acceptance that there is a problem

This proved to be the case, and the results were discussed at a senior management meeting, which included the headteacher. It was accepted that there was indeed a problem. Further discussion elicited that the school did have a written policy on bullying, but that not many staff in the school remembered having been involved in drawing this up, and there was a great deal of uncertainty about its contents.

Planning to involve different perspectives

It was therefore decided to start afresh, with one of the deputy heads as the main co-ordinator. This was a means of giving the project a high status, which would make success more likely. It was agreed that the co-ordinator would arrange to have a monthly meeting of a working group consisting of interested teachers, amongst whom should be at least one assistant teacher, one head of year, one form teacher and the special needs co-ordinator. Also, a parent representative of the school governors was invited, together with the education social worker and the educational psychologist. The co-ordinator would also liaise with the Pupil Council, which had been established in the school the previous year.

Involving the whole school community

The Anti-Bullying Working Group (ABWG) agreed that the most important starting point was to make the entire school community feel involved and to raise everyone's awareness of the problem of bullying. This was achieved by:

- a whole staff (teaching and non-teaching) development day on bullying;
- a series of themed assemblies;
- a competition to design anti-bullying posters;
- questionnaires, sent to both parents and pupils, on what they saw as bullying and what they thought could be done about it.

Establishing clear procedures for prevention and intervention

While the information was being collected and fed back in a summary to members of the school community, so that a definition of bullying could be established, the ABWG also clarified for itself what the school was already doing, in the way of both prevention and intervention when bullying occurred. This highlighted the need for clear procedures which spelled out:

- what pupils should do when they are bullied;
- what pupils should do when they know of someone being bullied;
- who in the school is the main contact for the pupils;
- what teaching staff should do when they notice any bullying;

- what teaching staff should do when a pupil tells them about bullying.

It took a considerable time to clarify this, but it was very worthwhile as staff, parents and pupils were all involved in these discussions, and so had a very clear idea of the content of the policy from the outset.

Consistent application of preventative and intervention procedures

Once these steps had been taken and information disseminated to the school community, the next step was to try to ensure consistent application of these procedures. It was decided that this would be possible only if the ABWG kept on meeting on a regular basis to assist in the process to keep everyone informed. A termly anti-bullying bulletin for the whole school was mooted as an idea and was taken up enthusiastically by the Pupil Council.

Writing the document, review and maintenance

Only when these points were clarified was it possible to put the anti-bullying policy into a written document which could go out to everyone involved. This was an opportunity for the school, twelve months after starting the process, to publicise the anti-bullying policy with some fanfare and awareness-raising. The policy was integrated into the school's existing behaviour policy.

Twelve months after the initial survey, the same one was repeated and showed a reduction of about 10 per cent in the number of bullying-type incidents.

- What other effective strategies could Ansfield School have used to involve everyone?
- How far is your school in the process of drawing up and reviewing its anti-bullying policy?
- What is the next step to be taken in order to help the process further along? What would the main obstacles be? With whom would these need to be discussed?

Box 6.3 Case study: planning, review and maintenance of the anti-bullying policy at Underham Junior School

In 1995, Underham Junior School started to measure bullying on an annual basis, using the Life in School checklist (see Appendix). After an initial drop in the first year, the level of bullying started to increase again gradually, year by year. In 1998, it was decided to select bullying as one of the areas for target-setting. It had been noted that the Year 4 children had reported a particularly high level of bullying that year.

The targets were as follows:

- to reduce recorded levels of bullying across the whole school in 1999 to below the overall level recorded in 1998 – i.e., below 15 per cent.
- to maintain the improvement in 2000;
- to reduce the recorded level of bullying in Year 5 in 1999 to below the figure for Year 4 in 1998;
- to maintain this improvement in 2000.

The school increased supervision in the yard during playtime. Children at risk of being bullied could be referred to senior management by the midday supervisors. Children were encouraged to use a quiet area of the playground and a special football area was set aside. A youth worker was invited into the school to come and work with the Year 5 children. A week of assemblies and half a day in Health Week were devoted to bullying.

In 1999, the school's Bullying Index reduced to 9, equal to the best figure achieved since records were begun. This was maintained in 2000 (see Table 6.1), after putting together a further action plan. For 2001, the opening of a new classroom was to give everyone more space in the school; a new garden would incorporate a quiet area; and there would be an extra midday assistant and extra teaching staff. The school also intended to develop a Schools Council, in order to encourage more pupil involvement. The Year 6 cohort would be targeted, as their Bullying Index was relatively high compared with the other year-groups. Staff were hopeful that these developments would lead to further reductions in bullying.

- How could your school measure and evaluate the work done on anti-bullying?
- Who needs to be involved in a discussion of this?
- Who needs to know your results?

Table 6.1 Bullying indices in subsequent years at Underham Junior School (illustrating use of Life in School checklist to monitor levels of bullying yearly)

Year	1995	1996	1997	1998	1999	2000
Bullying Index	11	9	12	15	9	9

- Does your school include the reduction of bullying as a target in its school development plan?
- How can you ensure that this happens on an annual basis?

Conclusion

This chapter has reviewed at length the many aspects of whole-school policies that school experience and research have shown to be important in combating bullying. One of the positive incentives some schools have given for starting and maintaining their anti-bullying policies is that this topic gives a really good opportunity for involvement of the children themselves in processes to improve behaviour in school. It also provides a conceptual framework to reduce many of the small tensions and incidents that take up so much teacher time each day. The one lesson from experience essential to observe is not to take short-cuts with the process of establishing the policy – formation of the project group, awareness-raising, consultation across the school and with parents on content of the policy, specification of the class-level and individual-level procedures, preparation and approval of the policy by all the groups involved in their respective meeting forums, dissemination, monitoring by repeat surveys on an annual basis or by other quantitative methods, and formal review. Taking short-cuts results in a much weaker policy which will have less impact both in the short term and over time.

Some questions to think about

- Which are the most important points of intervention to ensure the sustainability of effective policies?
- Given the rate of turnover of school staff, including senior management staff, which is the most appropriate group of people to review anti-bullying policies? What is the essential information they need, and to whom should they report?
- How can schools work with parents most effectively in combating bullying? Should this be only in the context of the anti-bullying policy?
- Should LEA staff or OFSTED expect schools to be operating the same anti-bullying policies?
- What is the relationship between a 'telling' school culture, where students do not hesitate to inform staff of bullying incidents, and successful anti-bullying procedures?

Chapter 7

Preventing and responding to bullying behaviour

Whole-school interventions

An emphasis on peer support

The importance of peer-led intervention is a consistent theme in anti-bullying programmes and one that makes sense when the social context of bullying is considered. Peers can be positively and effectively involved in tackling bullying behaviour in schools. This can be achieved in a number of ways, through:

- participation in the establishment of a whole-school anti-bullying policy;
- the development of their own solutions to the problem of bullying;
- the encouragement of positive relationship management and active bystander behaviour;
- the provision of a listening or befriending service for peers who are bullied.

Given the nature of bullying behaviour, including the peer group in the design and implementation of anti-bullying strategies seems essential. This chapter follows those elements of pupil involvement used in schools that were successful in reducing bullying.

Involving pupils in the development and implementation of a whole-school anti-bullying policy

In the successful Sheffield schools, the schools' anti-bullying policy clearly defined the role that peers should play in the prevention of and response to bullying behaviour. A variety of peer-centred intervention strategies were established in order to put the policy into practice. Although the school staff retained ultimate responsibility for ensuring the welfare of pupils, an understanding of the nature of bullying behaviour led schools to recognise that it would more often be peers than staff who witnessed bullying behaviour. Any effective response to bullying therefore had to include initial action by peers in alerting appropriate adults and in discouraging the continuation of the behaviour. Prevention would depend upon all members of the school community, including pupils, overtly disapproving of bullying behaviour and actively promoting acceptance, tolerance and constructive management of difficult relationships.

Curriculum-based approaches

The curriculum is one of the most effective vehicles for teaching students how to prevent and manage aggression and violence in their relationships. The curriculum can be used to raise awareness of the types of behaviours classed as bullying and the problems these can cause. This enables teachers to introduce the subject of bullying and aggression and explore what they are and how they affect us, etc. By itself, it is unlikely to lead to long-term change in student behaviour, but it can form an effective part of a whole-school approach. For example, Fonzi *et al.* (1999) describe an awareness-raising programme during which pupils used a story about bullying to stimulate discussion about the impact of bullying, including their own experiences, and explored through role-play the physical and emotional consequences of bullying. The programme was carried out for one or two hours a week over three months and led to greater awareness of the impact of bullying behaviour.

The curriculum can also be used to intervene and actively to teach students how to manage their relationships more constructively. This requires long-term programmes of study, including skills such as assertiveness and conflict resolution. These need to be reinforced throughout the curriculum and throughout the school community. Curriculum interventions can be used also to explore the impacts of bullying and other antisocial behaviour.

There is a wide range of resources available to schools for curriculum-based work on bullying. These include videos, plays, poetry and fiction. Alison Skinner's *Bullying: An Annotated Bibliography* (1992) provides an excellent overview of these. There are also organisations such as the National Association for Pastoral Care in Education which, in conjunction with the Calouste Gulbenkian Foundation, has set up a library of materials relating to bullying behaviour.

Materials for awareness-raising can be used as the basis for discussion, drama, role-play and creative writing about bullying behaviour. They can be used to explore issues such as the following:

- What is bullying?
- What causes people to bully each other?
- How does it feel to be bullied/to bully?
- What are the effects of bullying behaviour on bullied pupils; on the pupils who bully others; on bystanders?
- What would our school and our society be like if bullying behaviour was acceptable?
- Why should we try not to bully each other?
- What can we do to stop bullying?
- What moral dilemmas do we face when we encounter bullying behaviour?

Episodes from history, politics and religious education can be used to illustrate incidents of bullying behaviour in a broader social context.

Raising awareness of bullying behaviour and the school's anti-bullying policy requires probably between two and three hours of curriculum time in any year. However, to maintain awareness and to challenge and change behaviour or attitudes needs a more prolonged and intensive effort. Schools who are serious in their attempts to tackle bullying effectively will need to reinforce anti-bullying messages regularly throughout the school year, as well as making them an ongoing theme in lessons and assemblies. Using teaching methods that actively promote co-operative behaviour and citizenship is one way of achieving this. One secondary school used the following themes in each year's pastoral programme to ensure that tackling bullying remained a constant theme:

Year 7: understanding bullying and our policy on it;
Year 8: tackling prejudice and harassment;
Year 9: assertiveness skills;
Year 10: conflict resolution;
Year 11: preventing bullying in the workplace.

Teaching pupils to manage their relationships constructively

Effective personal relationship skills are learned and can be improved with practice. Some bullying will occur because pupils have not learned alternative ways of handling problematic relationships and the feelings that such relationships arouse. Sullivan (2000) summarises various ways of handling problem situations in school through group work with children. DeCecco and Richards (1974) found that many of the 8,000 students included in their study ignored or avoided conflict situations. This suppression of anger often led to a build-up of tension and outbursts of misdirected violence. Johnson and Johnson (1989) found that children were often unable to manage conflict in a positive and constructive manner. Their research showed that conflict was frequently dealt with by employing bullying behaviour: teasing and insults, put-downs, or by referring the problem to someone with more authority and power to 'sort the other person out'.

Children and young people can be taught how to resolve conflict themselves and how to mediate for others (Kreidler 1984; Kingston Friends 1987; McCaffrey and Lyons 1993). Bryant (1992) demonstrated that children who deal with conflict calmly and constructively develop better peer relationships than those pupils who respond by being aggressive or by avoiding the situation. Where conflict resolution and mediation skills are taught and used in school settings, interpersonal relationships are enhanced among the pupils and between teachers and pupils.

Essential skills for effective handling of conflict are assertiveness and active listening. Within the Sheffield project, pupils who were identified as being persistently bullied were taught how to make assertive statements, how to resist manipulation and threats, how to remain neutral and calm in bullying situations, and how to enlist support from bystanders. Evaluation of this training indicated that pupils who had taken part felt more confident, experienced increased self-esteem, and used more constructive coping strategies in difficult situations (Tonge 1992; Childs 1993). An important feature of this training was the combination of teaching self-help strategies to pupils who were targets of bullying behaviour and working on the policy and bystander roles to raise the sensitivity of peers. When pupils used the assertive strategies they were more likely to be supported by peers and therefore their response was more likely to be effective.

Establishing quality circles

Within the DfEE Sheffield anti-bullying project (Smith and Sharp 1994), some primary schools used quality circles (QCs) as a method for involving the peer group in the development of anti-bullying strategies. The idea of the quality circle comes from industry, where they were initially implemented as a means of engaging employees in participative management approaches. Essentially, a quality circle is a small group of individuals who meet regularly to follow a structured problem-solving process. The members of the quality circle identify concerns and problems that directly or indirectly affect their work. One of these is selected, the nature and extent of the problem is explored, and a solution is developed. This solution is presented to management and, if appropriate, is implemented (Sharp and Smith 1994).

The effectiveness of the QCs was evaluated in the Sheffield project through observation of QC work in practice in three primary class-rooms as well as teacher and pupil interviews and questionnaires (Mellor Smith 1992). The success of the QC work seemed to relate to the participative nature of the approach. The pupils perceived that they were engaged in working collaboratively with peers on real problems and that their solutions, if practical and realistic, would be implemented throughout the school. To enable the QCs to be successful, both the school and the class teacher needed to be committed to enabling the pupils to take a participative role in school management. This meant that the adults in the school community had to be prepared to share power and decision-making with the pupils by respecting and recognising the value of their solutions.

In a survey of fifty-seven pupils' attitudes towards participation in a QC (Mellor Smith 1992), over half of those who took part stated that they had become more aware of bullying and that they now tried to stop it; 69 per cent said that they were more careful about what they said and did to others at school.

Typical pupil responses included:

- 'QCs show that we can take an active role in preventing bullying.'
- 'They help pupils to improve their own environment.'
- 'They make you more aware of the damage that bullying can cause.'
- 'It feels as though you are really in charge . . . we stop bullying

... we've been doing it for two years ... it makes the school better.'

There is no evidence to suggest that QC work on its own will stop bullying behaviour, but the research indicates that it enables pupils to investigate the issues meaningfully and provides them with a clear structure to formulate and implement their own solutions. It raises awareness about the problem of bullying and helps pupils to understand and reflect upon their own behaviour and attitudes towards others. Its basis in a co-operative learning style promotes a non-violent, constructive approach to problem-solving. It does need time to achieve this, and this has to come from somewhere else in the school day. Box 7.1 illustrates the successive steps in problem-solving during the QC.

The pupils work in groups to identify common problems, evolve solutions and present these solutions to 'management' (the class teacher, senior management team or governors). The pupils are taught specific skills and strategies for problem-solving and effecting change. These include skills for generating ideas, observation and data collection, the development of strategies or solutions, and communication both within the circle and when presenting to management.

The outcomes of the QCs are usually practical and can be implemented by the pupils themselves. For example, in one project school a QC identified that a major cause of bullying was boredom at playtime. They planned and organised a games tournament to occupy pupils during the lunch hour. Another QC felt that the root cause of relationship problems was lack of recognition for co-operative behaviour. They designed a reward system that became part of the school's approach to behaviour management.

Teaching pupils how to challenge bullying behaviour

A central element of curriculum-based work is empowering pupils to tackle bullying themselves. Pupils in the nursery and upwards can be taught, by the use of assertive scripts, to refuse to comply with the bullying pupil's demands. This is simply teaching young children what to say and do when other children attempt to bully them. The curriculum material may be stories, written or oral, or dramatic role-play.

Box 7.1 The quality circle process

Step 1: identifying and prioritising the problem

The members of the QC identify all the problems they encounter and select one to tackle first. Techniques here include brainstorming, frequency counting, or simple voting.

Step 2: analysis of the problem

The pupils consider possible causes of the problem, breaking these down into identifiable contributors, and select the key causes. They then establish the extent of the problem by collecting data about it. Useful techniques include carrying out a survey (for example, on name-calling or kicking in the playground), interviewing a sample of children about experiences of being bullied, or making selected observations during an agreed time-slot (for example, between noon and 1 p.m. on a Friday) of behaviour in a particular area of the playground (for example, behind the bicycle shed).

Step 3: developing a solution

The circle members suggest solutions. The 'how–how' technique is useful in exploring alternative solutions to a problem. Pupils suggest a possible solution and keep on asking themselves: 'How will this be achieved?' until they have broken the solution down into its smallest components and have identified a starting point for action. A plan is then formulated to implement this. A small pilot run is often useful to see if the plan works in practice. Preventative measures can also be thought out to ensure the problem stays solved.

Step 4: presenting the solution

The pupils prepare a presentation of their solution to 'management'. The solution 'belongs' to the QC members.

Step 5: reviewing the solution

If possible, 'management' helps implement the solution, evaluates how effective it has been, and feeds this back to the QC. If not possible, management must discuss with the QC why the solution cannot be implemented. The QC can then review their solutions in the light of these reasons or can move on to another area of concern.

The majority of pupils in the school may not be directly involved in bullying behaviour themselves, but they are likely to know that it is happening, and some may take an indirect role that colludes with or encourages the bullying. These bystanders may do nothing because they are afraid, uncomfortable or because they do not know what they should do. Schools will not want to encourage pupils to take on the role of vigilantes who 'stop bullying', but they can motivate peer pressure so that pupils take an active stand against bullying behaviour, and become 'defenders'. Pupils can be encouraged to challenge bullying by:

- not allowing someone to be deliberately left out of a group;
- not smiling or laughing when someone is being bullied;
- telling a member of staff what is happening;
- encouraging the bullied pupil to join in with their activities or groups;
- telling the bullying pupil to stop what he or she is doing;
- showing the bullying pupil that they disapprove of his or her actions.

Playground developments

Much bullying takes place outside the classroom, usually out of view of adults. This may be on the journey between lessons, in the toilets, the dinner queue, around the school grounds or on the way to and from school. Schools can reduce levels of bullying by:

- improving supervision;
- making changes to the school grounds.

Improving supervision

Effective supervision will involve moving around the school grounds, visually scanning the area to anticipate potential difficulties, and engaging in brief conversation with pupils. For younger pupils it may also involve staff directly initiating play activities. The emphasis in this section is on dealing with negative behaviour, but *too* much emphasis on the 'policing' aspect of supervision could negate what should be an enjoyable part of the day for pupils and hinder them developing important social skills.

If any teacher or supervisor suspects that there may be a problem concerning pupil behaviour he or she should investigate the situation straight away. This should be done quietly and calmly.

The most common barriers to effective supervision are:

- lack of clarity about the school's behaviour policy and the role of supervisors;
- lack of training in techniques to recognise and manage challenging behaviour.

Most supervision, whether carried out by specially employed supervisors or qualified teachers, can be improved, through discussion and training, to address these barriers. Schools need to establish a two-way method for efficient communication between supervisors and whoever is responsible for co-ordinating the school's discipline policy. They also need to clarify the roles and responsibilities of supervisors and teachers when on duty. In Box 7.2 the steps taken in the DfEE anti-bullying research project (Sharp and Smith 1994) to increase the communication with lunchtime supervisors are illustrated.

Box 7.2 Steps taken in the DfEE anti-bullying project to enhance the status of supervisors

- 'Teaching staff' meetings were for teachers; 'staff' meetings were for everyone.
- Supervisors were invited to attend staff meetings (especially those relating to behaviour or health and safety) and were given time to have meetings of their own, sometimes with a senior teacher, so they could communicate their ideas and views.
- Supervisors were included in working groups to tackle policy development concerning behaviour and discipline.
- Supervisors were invited to propose changes to the organisation of lunchtime that they felt would make the system more effective.
- 'Handover time' was introduced to facilitate effective communication between supervising staff and teachers.
- A clear system of rewards and sanctions was identified for use by the supervisors.

Even with a behaviour management system in practice, the authority of supervisors is not always acknowledged by pupils or teaching staff. This lack of status can undermine supervisors' efforts to manage pupil behaviour. Supervisors need to be able to operate rewards and sanctions for pupil behaviour, to refer an incident for further action if necessary, and to know how and when it has been followed up. They should be supported, rather than overruled, by teaching staff when asserting their authority.

Some supervisors have no experience of behaviour management techniques. If they are to implement the school's discipline and anti-bullying policy they may need to be taught these skills. This can give supervisors the confidence to handle difficult situations in the school grounds themselves. Teaching staff can share skills with supervisors through either school-based training, or mentor schemes which link teachers with supervisors or via regular meetings with supervisors, where they can discuss specific incidents and alternative ways of handling them.

In a supervisory situation, the adult is sometimes able only to observe interaction between pupils – she or he is not necessarily able to hear the content of the conversation. Sometimes, what looks like fighting or bullying can simply be rough-and-tumble play or 'play-fighting'; this is something that children usually enjoy. For effective intervention, however, it is crucial that the supervisors can differentiate between the two. Box 7.3 gives some distinguishing features.

Box 7.3 Differentiating between play fights and aggression

Children in play fights often:

* are smiling or laughing
* make 'mock' blows or kicks that do not connect, or only do so softly;
* take turns in being on top, or chasing the other;
* do so in the open, but are ignored by other pupils.

Pupils who are being attacked or physically bullied often:

* frown or look unhappy/angry;
* try to move away from the aggressor;
* do not take turns, the aggressor maintaining the dominant role throughout the interaction;

Improving the school grounds

Bullying will not disappear if the playground environment alone is improved but, equally, any number of interventions may be used to little effect if the physical environment does not support 'positive' play. A poor environment lacks diversity and stimulation and offers few settings for a variety of educational, social, physical and creative activities. A poor school ground environment leads to boredom, crowding, marginalisation and exclusion of games or groups of pupils. In contrast, a good school ground environment will be rich, diverse, flexible and multi-functioning, with specific settings, areas and features for a full range of play experience and teaching functions. It combines variety in greenery, colour and texture with security, safety, and ease of supervision and maintenance.

A planned approach to playground development is essential. A single, attractive new feature in the playground can create new problems of its own as all children compete for access, and it may well have a limited lifespan, have used up available funds and have no lasting impact. Playground improvement is a continuous process – the playground is never 'finished' – and it can be assisted by establishing a playground development group, with representatives of all stakeholders in the school community.

A good playground environment is divided into zones for different activities, which are separated by planting, fences or other features. Access routes and trails enable circulation as well as play opportunities. Murals, mosaics, floor paintings and sculptures offer stimulation as well as practical games opportunities. A variety of seating and edges enables children to spend time talking or playing stationary games.

Using group methods to work with the individual

One of the characteristics of bullying is that it is a social process. It exists as a part of the patterns of social life, and just as bullying emerges as a part of this, the social life of the group can be effective in replacing bullying with other patterns of relationships. Student group work can be used either to support the silent majority to challenge the acceptance of bullying in the group, or to support the victims and reduce the impact of bullying when it occurs. How can these group work processes be started in schools?

What can be done to tackle bullying at the level of the pupil group

All the research evidence seems to suggest that it is essential that we tackle bullying at the group level. General levels of bullying are influenced by organisational and group culture and are therefore extremely resistant to one-off or short-term individual actions. One key intervention will be the establishment of a whole-school policy, which is described in detail in Chapter 6. This gives an impetus to the development of an anti-bullying culture through describing organisational procedures to create both the policy statement and its accompanying culture. Then, within this culture, the series of individual actions by teachers and other staff, and by pupils them-selves, can maintain the culture and give a supportive environment for the specific interventions to influence directly both the bullies and the victims. This section focuses on peer-led interventions as an effective intervention strategy at the level of the pupil group.

Pupil involvement in establishing 'class rules'

In an extensive Norwegian project (Olweus 1991), an 'anti-bullying' charter was developed by each class in each school. Pupils were engaged in agreeing their own procedures for tackling the problem of bullying. Once the charter had been agreed, regular, class-based discussions about social issues affecting the peer group became part of the weekly timetable for pupils. In these class meetings any problems about bullying could be addressed. Levels of bullying fell by, on average, 50 per cent. The Sheffield-based project (Smith and Sharp 1994) found that pupils in schools which had included them in developing school guidelines for behaviour were more confident that staff took bullying seriously. In secondary schools in particular, higher levels of pupil involvement led to larger reductions in levels of bullying behaviour and an increase in the number of pupils willing to tell a teacher if they were being bullied.

Teaching pupils to challenge bullying behaviour

Latané and Darley (1970) established that helping behaviour is often inhibited by the presence of others. In a series of fifty-six experi-ments, people in a group situation only helped another in distress or difficulty 53 per cent of the time (Latané and Nida 1981) compared with 75 per cent of the time if a person on their own witnessed an incident. In the initial Sheffield survey (i.e. before any intervention had occurred), half of the pupils who completed the questionnaire said that they would not help another pupil who was being bullied, or that they would join in. Latané and Nida found that children less than 9 years old would still spontaneously help others regardless of who else was present. This sense of social responsibility can be encouraged and developed through teaching effective responses to bullying behaviour.

There are a number of ways in which pupils can indicate support for bullying behaviour, therefore colluding with and encouraging it. Pupils can passively support the bullying behaviour by ignoring it or by remaining silent when it does occur. These pupils can maintain the isolation associated with the victim's role by avoiding the bullied pupil(s) or by not inviting them to join their social group. They can socially reinforce the pupils who are carrying out the bullying by co-operating with them, being friendly towards them or by ignoring the bullying behaviour. They can even help to enhance the reputation of the bullying pupil by spreading rumours about bullying incidents. Pupils can more actively encourage bullying behaviour by verbally supporting the behaviour; preventing the pupil being bullied from escaping the situation; shielding the situation from adult view; acting as 'look out'; generally assisting the pupil to bully; directing the bullying behaviour; acting as a messenger for the pupils who are bullying; laughing or smiling at the bullying behaviour; writing graffiti which confirms the role of the pupil as victim or bully; refusing to give information about the situation even when asked. The consequences of these kinds of behaviour can be explored with pupils through role-play and discussion.

In the same way, more challenging behaviours can be taught and encouraged. Pupils who witness bullying taking place can get help from an adult; align themselves with the victim; indicate disapproval non-verbally; assist the bullied pupil to escape the bullying situation; directly challenge the bullying by making statements such as: 'That's not fair,' 'Leave her alone', 'If you don't stop I'll tell the teacher.' The moral dilemmas that accompany witnessing bullying behaviour can also be explored.

Making it explicit how pupils can respond effectively when they witness a peer being bullied and rehearsing these responses through role-play, increases the likelihood of pupils supporting each other when bullying does occur. Once pupils have understood how collusion reinforces bullying behaviour and how low-level resistance can prove extremely effective in stopping the bullying, they are more confident in taking an active role in tackling the problem. The long-term effect of this kind of peer intervention is the development of an anti-bullying peer ethos which operates alongside adult intervention and hinders the establishment of classes or groups where high levels of bullying behaviour are the norm.

Establishing social support structures

Social support reduces the negative impact of stressful and adverse situations, as has been outlined above. Social support may come from both adult and peer relationships. As we know that one of the common results of bullying is to leave the bullied child isolated within his or her peer group, intervention to increase social support is very important. Establishing a social support structure can range from appointing a 'buddy' from within the class group through to more formal interventions such as 'Circle of Friends'.

In Circle of Friends, a small group of peers is nominated from a larger one as supporters to a specific child. They agree how they will help the child to be included and supported over a period of time (Taylor 1996). Sympathy for the young person is first established by making the larger group aware of the feelings and distress he or she has been experiencing and how this could be linked to their behaviour. Ideas are then solicited from the group on how to help the young person, and volunteers are sought to put this into action. The volunteers then meet with the focus young person on a regular basis, under the supervision of a member of staff, to discuss targets and celebrate successes (for instance: 'How can we make sure that Anna is included in our activities at lunchtime?'). Circle of Friends has been used with children from 4 years of age to those in the secondary stage. Feedback from this type of intervention has generally been very encouraging. It may not only effect positive changes in the young person for whom it was set up in the first place, but can also be a useful learning experience for the volunteers and for others in the group. In Canada and North America, the Circle of Friends approach is widely used to encourage inclusion. More specifically, it is used routinely when a new pupil (especially one with special needs) is admitted to the school. In such cases, the need for schools to be more than 'curriculum transmitters' is acknowledged. Social relationships are as important as (and, some would argue, more important than) academic knowledge and ability. Without a feeling of belonging and being secure in a group, academic learning will not take place. Teaching young people to care, to show respect and to include others are essential skills and a logical part of an effective anti-bullying policy. Circle of Friends can provide one vehicle to help pupils practise such skills in a very real way.

Groups of pupil volunteers can also be trained to be 'befrienders', to be available at breaktimes and other times of the day, to listen or talk to other children. In some schools, these befrienders operate a 'friendship stop', which is a place set aside in the playground where children can sit and have a chat with others, or find a volunteer who will play with them.

Establishing a peer counselling service

Pupils are often resistant to discussing their experiences of bullying with an adult. Establishing a peer counselling service can provide a complementary network of support within the school context. A group of pupils is trained to provide a supportive context where bullied pupils will be listened to, taken seriously and where they will be helped to explore feasible solutions to their difficulties. The service runs at appropriate times during the school day, usually over lunchtime.

To date, most of the evaluative studies of peer counselling services have been based in Canada and North America, and none of these were specifically concerned with bullying problems. These studies suggest that, given appropriate training and support, pupils are very able to provide a caring environment for peers where their concerns are listened to and where they can explore possible solutions. There are benefits for pupils using the service, for the counsellors themselves and for the school as a whole (Carr 1988; Carty 1989; De Rosenroll 1989). Evaluation of a peer counselling service in one secondary school (Cowie and Sharp 1996) demonstrated that the service was perceived as helpful by bullied pupils, particularly by pupils in Years 7 and 8 and by pupils who had special educational needs. Usage of the service was highest in the first term of the new academic year. Naylor and Cowie (1999) have carried out a more extensive evaluation of peer support services across the UK. They found that the services were well used and valued by pupils, parents and staff. They also found that there were measurable benefits, in terms of improved self-confidence and self-esteem, for pupils involved in providing the service.

Although peer counselling services are an effective way of enabling pupils to support their peers, care must be taken in establishing and maintaining such a service. While the potential benefits are great, the potential for disaster is equally real. First, such a service should offer an extension of support rather than a replacement of adult roles: there will be some pupils who prefer to discuss concerns directly with an adult. In addition, running this kind of service has a number of ethical and organisational implications, in particular relating to confidentiality, responsibility, training and supervision.

Some assurance of confidentiality is necessary if other pupils are to feel secure to use the service. However, ethically the school is still obliged to monitor problems faced by pupils under its care. Pupils involved in the peer counselling service can therefore only offer semi-confidentiality – i.e., they will not discuss the other pupil's problems with anybody other than an appropriate member of staff or within a supervision session. A procedure must be established for any pupil who discloses abuse to a peer counsellor.

It is the school that ultimately holds responsibility for all pupils in its care. By establishing back-up systems the school can ensure that it remains aware of how the service is being used and that it follows up quickly any incidents when the counsellor has acted inappropriately or when the child using the service is experiencing serious difficulties. In such cases, the onus remains with the school staff to take direct action. Such incidents will be avoided by ensuring that the role of the counsellors is clearly defined.

The quality of training and supervision will determine the effectiveness of the service, and schools need to consider who offers such training. This person should ideally be an experienced counsellor him or herself, and it may be necessary for schools to involve local support agents such as educational psychologists or other professional trainers if nobody within the school has the necessary skills. The duration of a training programme will vary according to availability of trainers and timetabling within the school. Although initial training should cover the essential skills, an ongoing, long-term training programme can allow pupils to improve their practice and develop new skills over time.

Linked to an ongoing training schedule, there needs to be some provision for supervision. Most helping professions recognise the value of supervision meetings, which provide a forum for discussion of practice. Through supervision, the pupils can explore the difficulties they encounter and consider ways of developing their listening skills. Without it, inappropriate counselling styles may become entrenched, and pupils could be handling problems that are beyond their capabilities.

Pupil 'counsellors' need opportunities to practise good listening skills:

- showing attentive body language;
- listening for the messages and emotions underlying people's statements;
- paraphrasing what has been said;
- refraining from interrupting or directly offering advice;
- being comfortable with silence, anger and tearfulness.

They also need to be clear about the extent of their responsibilities, and have guidelines about confidentiality set down. To what extent can they help the bullied pupils? Who is responsible for working with the bullying pupils? What degree of confidentiality can the service offer? The pupil counsellors need to know what they should do if something goes wrong, or if someone is being physically or sexually assaulted or is involved in self-harmful activities (for example, drug taking). Pupils should keep some form of records to allow the school to monitor usage of the service.

Summary

Peer involvement in the prevention of and response to bullying behaviour is essential for effective intervention. It is peers who witness bullying behaviour; it is the peer group that creates and maintains the social context within which bullying behaviour can either fail or thrive.

Peers can be positively and effectively involved in tackling bullying behaviour in schools by:

- participation in the establishment of a whole-school anti-bullying policy;
- the development of their own solutions to the problem of bullying;
- the encouragement of positive relationship management and active bystander behaviour;
- providing a listening service for peers who are bullied.

Given the nature of bullying behaviour, including the peer group in the design and implementation of anti-bullying strategies seems essential.

Peer involvement has to be managed appropriately – it should be supported by adult intervention, closely monitored and seen as an extension, rather than as an alternative, to adult support. The ultimate responsibility for tackling this problem rests with the adults within the school community.

Attention should be given to the potential failure of peer support structures and for the possible implications of such an outcome for the pupils involved. It is improbable that any type of intervention against bullying will always be completely successful. Training for pupils as peer helpers should prepare them for the possibility of failure and help them to develop a range of back-up strategies for such an occurrence. Training should also emphasise the need for judgement within the immediate context. Pupils themselves must assess each situation they encounter and make a decision about the best course of action. When bullying is involved they must be encouraged to consider their own personal safety when choosing a response. There may be times when the most sensible solution is to get adult assistance as quickly as possible.

Finally, just as peer involvement must go alongside adult involvement, the role of the victims of the bullying must not be overlooked. If we fail to encourage bullied pupils to make their own response to the situation, we run the risk of reinforcing their sense of helplessness. Peer and adult intervention should aim to support bullied pupils to stop bullying from recurring as well as assisting the pupils who bully to relate more constructively to others.

Interventions for individuals

The last two sections have shown how interventions to reduce bullying can take place at the level of the whole school, to create the culture where bullying is recognised as a danger to individuals involved (bullies and victims alike), eventually threatening the social cohesion and effectiveness of the whole group; and at the level of the group, to influence the individuals who find themselves in bullying relationships. After both kinds of initiatives are underway, there will be a need to support the individual children who are directly involved in the bullying. Teachers have a duty of care to the children in school, and parents have considerable emotional investment in the welfare of their particular children, rather than the group to which they belong. What are they to do to react to the bullies and help heal the victims? If the problems are recognised, then doing nothing is not really an acceptable option for most adults.

Stopping bullying once it has begun

Successful methods employ a problem-solving approach. Teachers can often find themselves spending significant amounts of time trying to find out who has done what to whom. More often than not, this leads to conflicting accounts of events from the parties involved. Usually, the most vociferous accounts, making light of the incident, come from those whom the teacher suspects of forming the bullying group. A problem-solving approach enables the teacher to accept that there will be conflicting accounts of events, and moves everyone forward to focus on taking action to stop the bullying recurring. In the next part of this section two formal approaches to problem-solving are described. However, it is possible for teachers simply to say: 'I have heard what you both/all have said. Although I don't know exactly what happened between you, it is clear to me that you are not getting on with each other.'

Most pupils will feel able to agree to this, and therefore can be encouraged to pose effective solutions to stop the bullying and prevent it recurring in the future. It is important that the teacher sets a review date in the near future when he or she will check that the situation has improved, to take the responsibility out of the hands of the victim and signal continued adult involvement to the children doing the bullying.

Three methods are commonly used to combat bullying directly; two of these – the Method of Shared Concern and assertiveness training for bullied pupils – were used in the DfEE/Sheffield anti-bullying project. These are described below.

The Method of Shared Concern

This is a counselling-based approach, devised by Anatol Pikas in Sweden, for resolving bullying situations. It focuses on the children doing the bullying as well as on those being bullied, and is designed for situations where a group of pupils have been bullying one or more pupils on a regular basis for some time. The method uses a combination of a simple script with specific, non-verbal cues. Training and rehearsal are needed to ensure a thorough grasp of the technique.

The overall aim of the Method of Shared Concern is to establish ground rules that will enable the pupils to co-exist within the same school. It does not aim to create friendship between the pupils, nor to uncover the accurate details of the bullying situation. The method starts with a series of brief, individual 'chats' with each pupil involved, in a room which is quiet and where there will be no interruptions. The pupils doing the bullying are seen first. The talks are not confrontational; the premise is that there is a problem – it has been witnessed by others that the bullied pupil is unhappy and has experienced bullying. The teacher follows a structured script with each pupil leading to mutual agreement that the bullied pupil is unhappy at the present time and concluding by each pupil agreeing to help improve the situation in some way. The most common outcomes are that the other pupils will either leave the bullied pupil alone or stick up for or be friendly towards him or her.

There is then a 'chat' with the bullied pupil. This primarily involves being supportive, but for those who do contribute to their own problems – Pikas calls these children 'provocative victims' – it involves helping them understand that their behaviour, too, should change. A week later, there are follow-up talks to check on progress. When ready, a final meeting of all the pupils involved is held. This aims to reach public agreement for reasonable behaviour on all sides and to determine long-term strategies for maintaining co-operative behaviour.

The 'script' for pupils who bully is as follows:

Teacher: (calm and neutral voice): I hear you have been nasty to Sami.
Pupil: It wasn't me!
Teacher: Nasty things have been happening to Sami. Tell me about them.
Pupil: (Silence – teacher doesn't break in or prompt).
Pupil: Well, some of the others have been teasing him about his clothes. He's so scruffy.
Teacher: So Sami has been having a bad time in school.
Pupil: I suppose so.
Teacher: What can you do to help improve things for Sami?
Pupil: Me?
Teacher: Yes, you.
Pupil: (Silence – teacher doesn't break in or prompt).
Pupil: I suppose I could get the others to lay off him.

Teacher: Excellent. You do that over the next week. We will meet again next week to see how you get on.

This process is repeated with each of the pupils who are suspected of bullying. With the victimised child, the script is similar:

Teacher: I hear nasty things have been happening to you.
Pupil: Yes . . . some of the other boys keep teasing me. They have put rubbish in my bag, set me up for trouble with the teachers. They won't pick me for the team even though I'm good at football.
Teacher: So you've been having a bad time in school.
Pupil: Mmmm.
Teacher: OK. What could you do to help improve things?
Pupil: I don't know. . . . I've tried to ignore them and that doesn't work. I suppose I could hang around more with Satpal. He's really cool.
Teacher: Excellent. You do that over the next week. We will meet again next week to see how you get on.

The final meeting usually goes as follows:

Teacher: We are here today because over the last two weeks all of you have been trying to improve things for Sami . . . and you have been successful. I'd like each of you to tell the group briefly what you have done. Jason, we will start with you.
Jason: Well, I've just not called Sami any names.
Uzzal: I've let him join in football at lunch times.
Mark: I've let him be.
Sami: I've spent more time with Satpal.
Teacher: And how have you felt over the last couple of weeks, Sami?
Sami: Much better. It's been good.
Teacher: Well done to all of you. OK, we are here today to agree how we can make sure this continues. We are going to be in the same class together for the next four years so, although we don't have to be good friends, we do have to get on with each other. So what could you do to continue this improvement in your relationships?
Uzzal: We could carry on doing what we are doing now.

Pupils:	(Nod in agreement).
Teacher:	Good. What if the bullying starts again, what then?
Mark:	We could have another meeting with you.
Teacher:	What do the rest of you think?
Pupils:	(Nod agreement).
Uzzal:	In fact should we meet anyway at the end of term just to check?
Teacher:	Great idea, Uzzal. Let's arrange a time now.

This method provided schools with a reasonably effective method for stopping bullying as an early step in a graded response system. The teachers who used it emphasised the importance of following up the pupils involved to make sure the bullying had stopped. Sometimes they found that after a term the bullying started again or the bullying gang might target a different pupil. They reported that if the bullying gang did contain a pupil who was persistently involved in bullying, it was best to combine the method with some other specific action targeted at that child. The kinds of strategies they found helpful were involvement of parents or a change of class.

The method was used with primary- and secondary-aged pupils. Pikas does not recommend this method for children less than 9 years old. Project schools that used the method found that some older primary-age pupils cannot suggest ways for improving the situation. They need the teacher to take a more directive role.

The No Blame Approach

Another counselling method which stresses a non-punitive response to bullying has been developed in the UK by Barbara Maines, an educational psychologist in Avon, and George Robinson, from the University of the West of England. Known as the No Blame Approach, it has been used in primary, secondary and college environments since 1990. This method was not included in the DfEE/Sheffield anti-bullying project, but has been evaluated by the authors. It is similar to the Method of Shared Concern, and the training materials are easily accessible to schools (Maines and Robinson 1992).

The teacher meets the bullied pupil first and takes an account of his or her distress and upset to a group of peers including the bullying pupil, some colluders and bystanders. There are seven steps to follow to conclude and evaluate the process. Each pupil suggests a way in which they will change his or her own behaviour in the future.

The No Blame Approach does not require such intensive training as the Method of Shared Concern. Training is available through Inset and as a distance learning pack with a video presentation. It combines an active condemnation of bullying and the distress it causes with a pragmatic course of action in the all-too-common situation where there is no direct independent evidence of the involvement of the particular pupils as the perpetrators of bullying. Where there is such evidence, the usual sanctions on pupils acting in a bullying manner must be applied, especially if the bullying is serious in terms of its effect on the victims, or has been continuing for a long period.

Assertiveness training groups for bullied pupils

Assertiveness techniques as described here are for use in small group settings, but they can also be used with individual pupils, or introduced to whole classes within the school.

Assertiveness training is a set of techniques based on a philosophy of human rights. These techniques employ a standard formula and provide pupils with a clearly defined structure to use in any situation where they are feeling pressured to do something they do not want to or are being treated in a way they do not like. Assertive techniques encourage the use of clear, direct and honest messages and avoid interactions that are deliberately manipulative, threatening, intimidating or dishonest. They can provide a sense of security for the pupils – almost a shield against the nastiness of a bullying situation. Pupils feel more control and power, less anger or despair. They are encouraged to respond in a neutral but direct way that de-escalates the situation.

There are a number of different types of assertive statement: responsive, where you try to find out the other person's viewpoint; empathic, where you acknowledge the other person's feelings; discrepancy, where you point out what was agreed and what is happening now. The most effective when confronting bullying are: basic, a simple statement of what you do or do not want to happen – for example, 'I want you to stop calling me names'; or consequential, pointing out the consequences of continuing with the behaviour – for example, 'If you continue to call me names, I shall report you to the headteacher.' The student may need to repeat the basic statement two or three times, and must do so in a calm, clear and direct manner, regardless of how intimidating or threatening his or her tormentors are trying to be.

Staying calm in the face of aggression is easier said than done, and students will probably need to be taught stress management techniques such as physical relaxation, breath control or visualisation to help them to achieve these strategies in difficult situations (Tonge 1992; Childs 1993). An important feature of this training is the combination of teaching self-help strategies to pupils who were targets of bullying behaviour and raising the sensitivity of peers through work on the policy and bystander roles. When pupils did use the assertive strategies, they were more likely to be supported by peers and therefore their response was more likely to be effective. However, the training should also continue to emphasise the need to involve the adults, unless the victims are sure they can handle it themselves.

In the project schools, assertiveness training groups were used with both primary- and secondary-aged pupils. The groups ran for between six and eight weekly sessions, during which the pupils were taught how to:

- make assertive statements;
- resist manipulation and threats;
- respond to name-calling;
- leave a bullying situation;
- safely escape from physical restraint;
- enlist support from bystanders;
- boost their own self-esteem;
- remain calm in stressful situations.

Usually, one assertive technique was introduced per session. Plentiful opportunities for rehearsal of each technique were provided. Sometimes there was a need to work individually with some members of the group to assist them in fully establishing a technique. If you are going to run a group like this, encourage pupils to use their own situations to practise the techniques. Since bullying situations are often persistent – pupils may find themselves trapped in a similar situation time after time – rehearsal gives the pupils confidence to use the technique outside the group and allows them to experiment with different strategies. Teachers using the techniques in project schools found it important to provide plentiful opportunities to rehearse how to respond to bullying behaviour. These role-plays should include bullying outside school as well as in school. If pupils did not practise the strategies sufficiently they did not use them.

The younger the pupils are, the shorter the sessions should be and the smaller the group. The optimum time for Year 4 or 5 pupils was found to be 20 minutes, with a maximum of six or eight pupils. In the secondary sector, the groups can last from 45 minutes to an hour and a half. Group size should not exceed fifteen members. Once the group has met for the first time, no new pupils should be admitted; however pupils can at any time drop out.

Experience in the Sheffield/DfEE project schools was that pupils seemed willing to attend in their own time, although in some cases use of curriculum time was negotiated. A benefit of running the groups at lunchtime was that it was viewed more like a club than a withdrawal class. It also enabled pupils to be more honest about whether or not they wished to attend. Drawbacks of a lunchtime group were that it limits the time the group can run – by the time pupils have eaten their lunch there may only be 30–40 minutes left; it depends on teaching staff being willing and able to give up their time; and younger pupils can find it tiring to work through the lunch hour.

Within the group, the pupils can develop close, supportive relationships, so teachers need to pay attention to how to end the sessions. The last meeting should be carefully managed to emphasise the gains the pupils have made from the group but, at the same time, that it is time to draw the group to an end.

Evaluation in the Sheffield/DfEE project schools showed that assertiveness training *can* boost pupil self-esteem and self-confidence. The pupils did learn and use the techniques to respond to and avoid bullying situations. They became more assertive and less aggressive or passive in their relationships with other pupils. The gains the pupils made in these kinds of groups lasted longer if they were offered some kind of on-going support, albeit not as intensive as the group. A meeting once a term or a drop-in room for lunchtimes can maintain pupils' self-esteem and encourage them to put the assertiveness techniques into practice.

Developing effective coping strategies

Coping strategies fall into two groups:

- problem-focused coping strategies, which aim to find a solution to the situation or change something about the situation which will make it less stressful;
- emotion-focused coping strategies, which do not alter the situation but which help the individual to feel better about it.

The first stage of effective coping requires an assessment of the situation and then a decision about which type of response is most appropriate: problem focused or emotion focused.

Problem-focused coping requires:

- problem identification and analysis;
- goal setting;
- solution generation;
- implementation and evaluation of a solution.

Emotion-focused coping requires:

- realistic evaluation of the consequences of the problem;
- positive reframing of the situation;
- positive affirmation of self;
- appropriate expression of emotion and relaxation.

Both these types of programme can be seen as the guiding principles behind specific curriculum materials or procedures, such as the social skills materials produced by Warden and Christie (1997). Implementing both types of programme requires teaching staff who are comfortable with group work with children, involving active discussion and participation in the class. In practice, each school has to choose which of the various intervention methods can best be mounted. The interventions will need to be maintained over some years, through successive reviews and training organised by the anti-bullying project group, in parallel with maintaining the anti-bullying policy itself through review and dissemination to successive groups of students and staff. Staff time, particularly of staff with the specific training and interest in the area, is perhaps the crucial resource. The case study in Box 7.4 demonstrates how this was done in one school.

Conclusions

These, and some of the other methods of intervention discussed, may seem to be applicable to children other than those directly involved in bullying situations. In general, they are and this is, in fact, one of their strengths. They all have potential benefits for all children, whether or not they are involved in bullying situations, and so the question of selection of pupils should not be too tightly focused only on particular children thought to be at risk. Ideally, many of the

Box 7.4 Case study: combining the whole-school policy with interventions at group and individual level in Ansfield High School

When the staff at Ansfield High School were considering their procedures for dealing with bullying as part of their whole-school policy, they tended to think first in terms of how to discipline pupils who bullied. However, it soon became clear that there were other areas to consider as well, and possibly more profitably. The Anti-Bullying Working Group (ABWG) took into account the immediate needs of the school, which had become apparent not only through anecdotal evidence, but also through the initial questionnaires sent out to parents and pupils. The group agreed that the main concerns for the school for the next year were:

• how to make the pupils who bully change their behaviour;
• how to help the victims of bullying to cope better next time or to avoid being bullied altogether;
• how to support victims of bullying.

The ABWG then consulted widely and read the literature on bullying. It decided that the No Blame Approach might be a useful one to deal with incidents of bullying. The educational psychologist met with all the senior staff to watch and discuss the video and to appraise the approach's possible merits. They agreed that it might effectively change the attitude of children who bully to one of concern for the victim and that this could provide support for the victim as well as change the bullies. Some staff had reservations that it would not work with 'die-hard' bullies, so it was decided to use it on a trial basis with Year 7. The head of Year 7 reported later that the approach had been very successful with some cases and less so with others, but that it was certainly worthwhile to use the approach consistently with the younger age-groups. A 'befrienders' scheme, similar to the peer counselling service discussed in this chapter, was set up in Year 8. This provided support to all children in this year-group and also trained a smaller group of children in counselling and befriending strategies. Their skills could then be used as they progressed through the school. The scheme was introduced by LEA support staff, with one member of staff as the co-ordinator, who received appropriate training to continue the scheme in following years. For those victims who needed more help at an individual level, the assistance of the educational psychologist was sought. She suggested that some might wish to meet on an informal group basis to discuss their feelings and possible coping strategies and that a solution-focused approach could be used to help this process. This proved difficult to set up because of lack of time and resources, but the school has now applied for funding, so this may happen in the future. The educational psychologist also suggested that one particular pupil in the school, who had been a victim of bullying, might be helped by the Circle of Friends approach (see this chapter). This proved to be highly successful in enhancing the pupil's confidence and she has actually been seen to stand up to bullying in a very effective way.

- If Ansfield High's anti-bullying policy had been at the above stage, how could Anna (one of the girls in the case study in Box 4.1 – see p. 85) have been helped more?
- What features from Ansfield High's anti-bullying policy may be effectively introduced in your school?
- How supportive are the senior management in your school for the process of drawing up and reviewing the anti-bullying policy? Do they commit practical support? How actively are they involved?
- Are there any other areas you may wish to develop, for instance the curriculum or links with parents?

methods can, and should, be used with whole class groups. This enables the anti-bullying message to get to the silent majority, who are not normally involved but who have a good deal of influence on setting limits of acceptability on the general group behaviour of the students. Some of the more specific methods which do require the establishment of special groups, gain from having not only vulnerable children involved, and certainly not only children who are being bullied.

Some questions to think about

- When and how should adults become involved with anti-bullying strategies for younger pupils, remembering both that early-years children are learning how to handle aggression as a part of their social development and the danger of intervening too late in what is a difficult and covert area?

- How can the school encourage the maintenance of supportive school systems, such as peer counselling or curriculum involvement?
- Given our knowledge of the group dynamics of bullying, what kinds of interventions other than those described here might work to reduce bullying, and what theoretical perspectives would they be based on?
- Given our knowledge of the differences in the dynamics of bullying at different ages, at what ages would the various interventions described be most effective?
- As there are legal rules about appropriate responses to bullying where actual bodily harm results, at what point should the No Blame Approach be abandoned?

Chapter 8

Researching bullying: where are we now?

Introduction: questions to be asked

Many questions can be asked about bullying, and the preceding chapters have gone some way to beginning to answer some of them. We have reached a clear understanding of how to define bullying and, in particular, the relevance of defining it as a process involving other 'associates' of the bully as well as the main person. We have explored various methods of assessment of how much bullying takes place, and realised the crucial difficulties of attempting a general answer for a town, city or country. The average figures resulting from such exercises can, however, serve only to emphasise the importance of the problem, and are themselves crude generalisations that may not relate at all to any particular institution. Due to the variability in institutional cultures and de-facto definitions of bullying used, the only meaningful answers are those given for a particular institution. These show a widely varying incidence between institutions but seem much more stable over time inside the same institution. They can reflect the influence of particular groups of children in particular year-groups in particular schools (Arora 1994), as a particular year-group with an unusually high level of bullying works its way up the school. For the purposes of schools wanting to reduce levels of bullying, the methods of assessment described here can give a useful index of change. We also have evidence of the psychological and psychosomatic damage to children who are caught as victims, sometimes long-term and severe.

We know something of the difference between bullying at primary and at secondary school levels. The former is more widespread but easier to influence (Smith *et al.* 1999). We also have some idea of how children learn about aggression, and of how they learn to incorporate habitual ways of using or dealing with aggression into the ways they make relationships with their classmates. Their emerging personalities can either accept that some relationships will be structured by consistently aggressive patterns of behaviour, or reject this way of structuring relationships and learn to use more reciprocal patterns of assertion, where sometimes one partner gets his or her own way and sometimes the other does. Where physical aggression or the threat of it is not used to organise relationships, such mutual assertion and accompanying occasional withdrawal gives a much more appropriate alternative. Such a pattern of interaction based on assertion and turn-taking rather than aggression also gives a flexible base for further learning about the interactions in the adult world, where relationships are negotiated between adults based on a combination of social roles and how particular personalities find they can inter-relate. There is still much research to do in these areas, in particular learning how to encourage some students to build other social skills using assertion rather than aggression. Again, Duncan (1999) gives a recent graphic description of where some schools and communities have to start from.

We are beginning to understand how particular children can be predisposed to fall into the role of bully or victim. Key factors are the extent to which they learn how to use or manage aggression and assertion in their interpersonal life, as discussed above, and the extent to which they look to their peer groups for support. These early beginnings are very significant, as through early learned behaviours they develop more advanced social skills for communicating effectively with their peers, as well as with authority figures, such as teachers or parents.

We are also beginning to understand something of the ways in which successful interventions can work. These are by enlisting the cultural expectations of the wider institutions behind the rejection of harm to the victim through curriculum interventions, through classroom-based systems of rules of mutual respect, through the Method of Shared Concern and its derivatives as sanctions for those doing the bullying, and through the stressing of school-wide policies. These policies cover the school's definitions of bullying and how the school responds to bullying incidents. They also include the staff training routes to learn specific anti-bullying approaches, and policy review systems. Induction procedures for new staff and new groups of students should also be included. The research demonstrates the crucial importance of involving the whole staff in the derivation of those policies, in the first place to coincide with their views on institutional priorities. When the policies are implemented in the day-to-day turbulence of school life, effective implementation is dependent on the detailed knowledge of the staff and students of the details of the policy.

Unfortunately, research in this area also highlights the tendency for such school-wide policies to decay over a two- or three-year period. With this decay, the levels of bullying rise back up to the levels they were at before the intervention to reduce bullying and to set up the policy in the first place. We also know that when the levels of bullying do reduce over time in association with school anti-bullying programmes, the reductions tend to be in the milder forms of bullying rather than in the hard-core of bullying interactions. We know that even in schools that have tackled bullying very effectively, demonstrating year-on-year reductions, there are still about 5 per cent of children suffering from the more severe forms of bullying at secondary-school level. This is about one in every class, assuming small classes. In schools that have not instituted anti-bullying programmes, it is easy to find incidences of more than two per class – about 10–13 per cent.

What are the remaining questions to guide practice? They cover a number of areas, which will be detailed later in this chapter, but in outline they are:

- How can we identify children in the early years who may be predisposed to become victims or bullies later on?
- Having identified them, how can we provide suitable learning experiences that will steer their personality development into more typical patterns?
- How can we best train parents, carers and teachers to provide learning experiences both for the vulnerable children, to develop their confidence and social skills, and for the children who are using aggression too frequently as a standard technique to influence others?
- When children start school, what are the most effective practices the school can use to minimise the amount of bullying?
- How can schools best maintain effective anti-bullying procedures and policies over a number of years?
- How does one form of inappropriate use of aggression – bullying – relate to other forms of systematic aggressive behaviour – such as sexual harassment and racism – in school and out of it?

- How do effective anti-bullying policies relate to other forms of behaviour policies in school and to other policies concerned with how children behave to each other, such as anti-racism policies, anti-harassment policies, and other equal-opportunity policies?
- How does involvement in bullying activities at school level lead on to similar problems of getting on with other people in adult life?
- How can research demonstrate possible links between stable and relaxed behaviour patterns in children in school and the academic achievement of those children?

Underlying these are often two prior, very serious questions:

- how can academic researchers possibly have anything useful to say about such a complex phenomenon, which happens in the quiet corners of schools and is often apparently invisible to some staff in schools?
- How can educational practitioners working in schools possibly find the time and support to do watertight research in areas such as development and minimisation of bullying in schools?

By now, the reader will have considered the review of many of the issues in the above chapters and some of the answers may be becoming clearer. However, the role of research itself in clarifying bullying processes, the types of research which will be of most assistance, and the background necessary for the researchers to have, still need to be explored.

Different roles for researchers

Bullying is a complex phenomenon, being an aspect of complex social interactions involving aggression and the formation of social groups and identities. It reaches public knowledge through the informal social worlds of children in and out of school, sometimes resulting in grievous social pressures and emotional damage to those who find themselves to be victims. Because of the range of aspects of the bullying, it needs a range of researchers from a range of backgrounds to give information on how it can be understood and challenged. These rough groupings would be:

- That group of academic researchers who study the patterns of development of children, particularly those concerned with the development of social abilities, and the part played by aggression in the development of those abilities.

- That group of academic educational researchers interested in the way schools operate to support children and how schools and parents can deal with the social stresses in children.
- That group of professionals with research training employed as support staff in LEAs, usually educational psychologists, support teachers or advisers. These can sometimes come together to enable the LEA itself to support schools in developing anti-bullying policies and procedures, by all the usual ways in which members of these different professional groups support schools. This group can also be very effective in helping academic and school-based researchers to identify each other and in setting up supportive networks to enable both groups to do more effective research.
- That group of teacher researchers based in schools. These include serving teachers studying for a higher degree with the support of academic researchers for specialised help in research methodology and also, possibly, teachers taking a 'teacher fellowship' period, when the sponsor expects them to do research. The 'teacher fellowship' research role can be a very demanding one. Many fellowships have only a short period of operation (for example, a term rather than a year). This short period gives little time for accessing the research community for effective support if the teacher has had little or no formal training in educational research methods. In addition, beyond the question of assessment of the frequency of bullying, this research area is not an easy one.
- Academic researchers working on a completely school-based project, where they spend most of their time in schools and become accepted as one of the adults in school. This last group is only rarely involved.

Researchers in all these roles have contributed to the research so far but, in many ways, the most crucial groups are the school-based researchers, either teachers or academic staff based in schools for periods of time. The teacher researchers, in particular, often have little time to carry out research on the projects in which they become involved. Their contributions are essential, however, because the 'final testing' of the usefulness of methods of assessing the incidence of bullying, as well as the conceptual frameworks for understanding it, has to take place in the schools. In addition, when research studies attempt to assess which anti-bullying methods are most effective in schools, the contribution of school staff operating in a research role is essential.

As the questions posed by research into bullying become more complex, and as the methods become more sophisticated, it seems likely that most future successful research will be done by collaboration between researchers from across the groups. Working together, such teams will be able to give methodological sophistication and support, skilled observation of the bullying context, and access to the context where bullying occurs. It is possible that LEA staff may enable small teams to form, or that academic researchers form teams directly with practitioner researchers.

Levels of knowledge of bullying

Bullying is a complex phenomenon and, in many ways, one of the first achievements of research in this area is to clarify which levels of knowledge are necessary to understand what is happening. In essence, these are detailed below.

How the patterns of normal development include development in managing aggression

This has been studied as a part of developmental psychology for a number of years, almost always by academic psychologists. Up to the mid-primary years, the research tends to use observational and experimental methods, sometimes taking place in natural school or pre-school settings (for example, Pepler and Craig 1995). One of the general problems with interpreting this area of research is that it tends to be reported for academic audiences, in academic journals and language, and very often in terms of the particular project which is being discussed rather than in terms of the implications for the wider community of parents or teachers. The development of theory from such research tends to be narrowly focused on the empirical results and tends to be expressed in the concepts of a particular academic theoretical position, rather than in terms which would make sense to a practitioner audience. This is a major limitation of the impact of the research, as this impact must always be mediated through teachers' understanding of the ways in which children learn to handle aggression. This essentially needs a good theory, well taught during teacher training as a priority topic.

However, some bullying takes place at secondary level and forms a part of the very complex patterns of adolescent interaction. This setting tends to be much more resistant to experimentally conceived approaches, due to the sheer complexity of the subject, apart from the difficulties of assessment of aggression and patterns of interaction in a school setting. Many psychologists studying aggression are used to using a 'positivist' approach, where a piece of behaviour is studied in an idealised form in an attempt to give research results which can be said to be true for a range of practical situations. Those studying aggressive adolescent interactions, however, are more used to using qualitative methods and an 'interactionist' model for describing the results of the research. These results are more in the form of description of models of possible psychological processes in the individuals, and patterns of interaction between individuals which may occur under certain circumstances, rather than working towards one theoretically rigorous and complete model from which predictions can be made. The search for the theoretically rigorous universal model is seen by many as a search for a will-o'-the-wisp, given the complexity of the world of adolescence, and its susceptibility to new patterns of social behaviour. When theoretically rigorous models of social aggression in adolescence appear, they are likely to be in a form which relates to concepts such as the development of identity and to be based on qualitative research methods. They also rely on the practitioner having a fairly sophisticated understanding of the various theoretical possibilities and choosing the most appropriate. Duncan (1999) gives an excellent description of how far we have progressed in this area, and the very lack of clearly defined multiple models resulting from this research gives an indication of how much further we have to go. It is quite possible that conceptual models based on experimental studies in younger children will play a large part in qualifying and elaborating qualitative models used at secondary level.

An alternative approach to understanding bullying behaviour – social information processing

One difficult question for researchers has always been to explain the mental state of the students who bully and, in particular, to establish how sophisticated their social skills are. If researchers could show that in some way students who bully perceive the social world in a different way to the majority of pupils, then it might be possible to re-educate them to make their transition to less-aggressive responses easier. Sutton (2001) and Sutton and Keogh (2000) explain in detail how questions might be asked in this area and summarise recent research which might contribute to the development of this line of thinking. Sutton also highlights another issue which teachers in school are well aware of – that children who bully are often different from each other, and explanations which relate well to one individual might be much less relevant to understanding another. Are we to try to understand the phenomenon of bullying, so as to be able to understand how best to approach children who bully, or should we concentrate on increasing our understanding of the way individual children develop and the specific impacts of specific experiences on them as individuals? Or do we have to attempt both?

Encouraging positive social interaction

The second major area is that of the development of positive social interaction between children – what psychologists call 'prosocial' behaviour. There has been much work in this area in recent years, and its importance for anti-bullying programmes is that it should give a theoretical and empirical description of how to encourage as many children as possible to develop the skills which will make them resistant to exploitation as victims. It should also enable teachers and parents to give those children wanting to be leaders and to be the centre of social groups the skills to achieve this without basing such leadership on techniques of systematic aggression. Like the first area, this will be much easier to achieve at primary level than at secondary level, due to the greatly increased complexity of social life during adolescence. This knowledge area is also likely to be constructed in the same way as the previous one, with the conceptual structures derived from primary-phase work being modified and extended to support the more person-centred conceptual structures necessary to produce useful models of social interaction for adolescents. It will be important for all researchers to recognise the change of theoretical research model necessary at the beginning of adolescence – to criticise models of adolescent development based on self-identity and self-esteem because they cannot give the generalisable predictions expected of experimental approaches with earlier age-groups, will be to miss the point entirely. In due course, research into the post-primary phases of development may well extend to use oral history methods, where the experience of particular individuals is examined in great detail to identify critical incidents which have had a great impact on the student concerned.

This area has had some very useful developments in recent years, with at least two significant research achievements which should be much more widely recognised. These are the projects reported by Cowie *et al.* (1994), to enhance the development of friendships between children in middle schools, and the work by Warden and Christie (1997) and Christie and Warden (1997), where the results of academic studies on the development of prosocial behaviour are expressed as programmes of work for teachers. These are good examples of initiatives where the next research efforts should be to replicate the evaluations of the effectiveness of the programme in schools and to discover what the crucial features are for successful implementation of the programmes. Both projects, incidentally, could be extended to begin to include metacognitive elements – the extent to which the children can incorporate their changes in friendship patterns into their views of themselves.

Description of other patterns of aggression in schools

Bullying came to the forefront of research interest in the UK because of the significance of parental and social concerns, not because of active choices by researchers. The whole topic is so complex that academic researchers need the active support of practitioner researchers and of the educational professionals to make much progress. There are other, similar patterns of aggression in schools that share similar characteristics and, under certain circumstances, may be said to overlap significantly with bullying. The four most obvious of these are:

- sexual harassment, and behind this the whole role of assertion and aggression in establishment of gender relationships;
- the development of aggressive relationships between the minority ethnic communities themselves, and between them and the majority ethnic group or groups;
- the development of aggressive relationships between young people and representatives of social authority;
- the aggressive roles for some pupils in some friendship groups formed in school.

These aggressive relationships have to date mostly been tackled from the social, psychological and sociological points of view. At some point, if the role of aggression in social relationships is to be understood, the psychology of the individuals and how they join together as groups need to be more researched. Much of the popular understanding of aggression at present is on the basis of responses to aggression in children and others taken by therapists of various kinds. It can be caricatured as either 'let it all hang out to get it out of your system', from some therapeutically inclined positions, or as 'learn how to control yourself', to limit and manage anger within certain social limitations, with a high regard for the value of sanctions in reducing aggression. At the level of social psychology and sociology, the interest has been on how aggressive patterns of behaviour become established. Researchers have also been interested in how expressions of aggression are understood between the rival groups and how they are managed or manipulated to avoid too much general social damage but still give small advantages to particular groups. Aggression is also sometimes seen as ritual displays, focused on maintaining some aspect of the group structure rather than taking its prime significance from the effects on the individuals. Teachers and parents deal with individual children who are in groups with other children, and they need conceptual frameworks (based on some empirical data) which link the skills of dealing with aggression with the development of self-identity and emotional independence in relation to group membership.

Studying the ways schools implement anti-bullying programmes

At present, we know something of some ways to influence the incidence of bullying and to treat both children who bully and children who are victims, and we have some knowledge of the way schools put anti-bullying programmes into practice. We also know, unfortunately, that some schools start off with higher levels of bullying, and seem to have poorer results from their programmes, than other schools do. We also know that, in many schools, the effect of the anti-bullying programmes gets less over the years, whilst in other schools the effect becomes greater. Much of the knowledge about the effectiveness of intervention programmes comes down to understanding more about the way in which the school as an organisation reacts to the challenge of implementing the programme and reviews it from year to year.

Specific questions for future research

Many of the developing general research areas identified above will need to be continued, in order to reach the point of clear conclusions or to recognise that the very lack of clear conclusions may be leading to the general understanding that this approach is unlikely to be fruitful. Some of the newer emerging areas are addressed below to try to stimulate discussion of the possibility of a new direction in anti-bullying research. These are:

- to explore if early identification is possible of children who may become either children who bully or children who are bullied – this is also related to how effective early intervention programmes might be;
- to construct a range of specific theoretical approaches or models to understanding the phenomenon of bullying, bearing in mind that different theories are likely to be needed to deal with the range of social situations in which bullying occurs – some different theories, which may develop into models, have been touched on above;
- to establish which methodological approaches for research work best in which type of situation, and for which type of question;
- to establish which are the most effective methods of training parents and teachers to recognise bullying processes, and to intervene to limit them;
- to establish how effective anti-bullying procedures in schools are best maintained, in the full 'busy school' context;
- to establish more details about any continuities between bullying in school and bullying after school, in terms of whether the same individuals are involved in similar patterns of behaviour.

Early-years identification and intervention programmes

At this age, fully formed patterns of bullying and victimisation are unlikely to be developed. However, some children will be beginning to show signs of frequent and increasingly inappropriate use of aggression in social relationships, and it is possible that some children may be on the receiving end more frequently than would be expected from a random distribution of aggressive interactions round the class. Research into just how early stable patterns of bullying do emerge would be very interesting. Evidence to date seems to suggest that by the age of 6, many children are aware of the danger of being victimised by classmates (Hazzan 1991), but this by itself would not confirm that stable patterns of bullying do exist. Intervention programmes based on increasing social skills to develop friendships and on managing group interactions without undue use of aggression, would be effective both to minimise exposure to bullying and to support the development of emotional and social competence in schools. It might also put on the educational agenda the issue of making a systematic educational effort to limit aggression in schools as a normal part of life for all children, even if the aggression was not actually a part of bullying patterns of behaviour at this stage. This would mean, however, a commitment to spend valuable time on social and emotional education for all young children.

Many educationists, however, and possibly many parents too, might resist the idea of spending valuable time and staff resources on increasing social competence for all children, when the same resources might be devoted to the search for academic attainments instead. One response to these worries might be to learn to stress existing teaching methods which can develop social skills and language skills at the same time – for example 'circle time' teaching methods. Social learning does not have to be at the expense of academic learning – in fact, for most children, the aim of academic learning is eventually to operate as adults in a social world, where well-developed communication skills are crucial.

If these social, competence-based styles of anti-bullying programmes are not given some priority for all children, then the only option is to wait for the bullying patterns to establish themselves, identify those involved and implement programmes for only those involved when their need is obvious. This delays the start of programmes and maximises the difficulty of delivering the social skills programmes, as the individuals have to be identified, their immediate stresses dealt with in terms of discipline and short-term support, and then the longer-term social skills training put into practice for these children alone.

Over the years, there has been much work done on changing the behaviours of pre-school children, in the generally desired directions of greater stability, less anxiety, more confidence, and less aggression. These programmes have taken place both in 'normal settings', for whole groups of children of similar ages, and in 'specialised settings', where usually one child is identified and given a specific programme of treatment by health or educational professionals. Both of these approaches have been carried out under different theoretical frameworks, ranging from parental support to change the ways parents interact with their children, to very specific programmes based on behaviourist theory for specific, 'clinical' conditions, where the individual child's behaviour has been identified as a problem. To be successful at this age, the 'specialised setting' programmes need to be well implemented and followed through into the periods after the interventions, and into the child's daily life. Generally speaking, when programmes are effectively implemented it is common to find positive change taking place in the children's emotional reactions. The bigger problem is usually to involve the family and other supporting institutions in the changes, so that they can continue to treat the child differently and maintain the progress after the outside professionals have withdrawn. Only then can the changes be said to have succeeded properly and, regrettably, in practice, this is the point at which problems begin to recur and the research reports go silent. This particular problem, of lack of maintenance of the positive changes in children's behaviour from the specialised circumstances of the programme into the normal conditions of living, also affects specialist treatment programmes at other ages. It is one of the reasons why many professionals tend to prefer to concentrate on achieving change in the normal situation to start with, and why programmes aimed at improving social behaviour by whole-group teaching are to be preferred, if they are available. Such situations also provide an opportunity of developing whole-group values supporting alternatives to aggression and ensure that the normal carers and teachers are centrally involved in and trained for the programmes from the beginning.

   In the early school years there are suitable programmes which can be implemented by teachers in school as a part of normal lessons (Warden and Christie 1997). The effectiveness of these programmes varies depending on how well they are implemented, and so there should be further research evaluating their effectiveness in a school context. Most programmes will influence a wider range of social behaviour than that directly involved in bullying situations, so the evaluations should be broad enough to include other types of social interactions. Methodological problems of isolating the effects of programme implementation from the other influences in children's lives at a very receptive age will make life difficult for researchers. In later school years there have been a number of evaluations of interventions, both in the normal teaching programmes as curricular interventions and of special groups set up to influence both victims and bullies. These interventions have been described earlier. However, more research on exactly how the interventions influence children's behaviour, the best ways to implement them, and ways of maintaining their effects would add greatly to knowledge, and would increase the effectiveness of the efforts of school staffs and supporting professionals.

Methodological approaches

Quantitative approaches

These research explorations in new areas need to work with ideas and theories that relate to the possibility of change for the children concerned through intervention programmes. For example, research studies relating to the extent and direction of changes which are part of normal psychological development – such as development of relationships with others of the same age, or the development of understanding in children about aggression in their social life, or ways of recognising and dealing with stress – will be of more use than studies relating the incidence of victimisation to class variables. Some research will be difficult to do except as part of large surveys. In small-scale work with small sample sizes, the research needs to identify the individuals involved as victims or bullies, and this will be, in effect, where individual children are willing to say anonymously that they have either been bullied or bullied others. In small studies it will be very difficult for the researchers to claim that the numbers of children identifying themselves are representative of the 'true' numbers of such children in the population considered. In a large study, on the other hand, with hundreds of children involved, enough bullies and victims will form part of the sample naturally for quantitative conclusions applicable to this population to be drawn from the data. There may still be a bias in the figures resulting towards overestimation or underestimation of the characteristics of the sample, but this should be a systematic bias over time, where the degree of error would remain the same and in the same direction. This will be even more the case if the survey is, in fact, a complete population survey of a meaningful group of children – for example, a complete primary school, or a year-group in a secondary school, where data are available in the literature to claim that this population is likely to be different from other similar groups in the incidence or characteristics of the bullying occurring. The difficulties of establishing the representativeness of a sample and accurately identifying the children being bullied and those doing the bullying, are likely to appear in research using quantitative methodologies in small studies. The effect is likely to be to encourage the researcher to use qualitative approaches in these small studies, or to choose longitudinal, single-case studies, where a mixture of methods can be used. The use of remote audio-visual devices (e.g. radio microphones) may make small-sample or individual-based observational studies easier, but may also raise ethical questions (Pepler and Craig 1995).

Qualitative approaches

Interpretative qualitative methodologies have the advantage of being more able to respond to the details of accounts given by individual informants. They are less dependent on researchers asking the right questions and, through new conceptual developments, are more likely to lead to new types of understandings of the processes involved. Such methods are particularly useful in research where the researchers' understanding of the experiences of the informants is not clear, and may be very relevant to clarifying the significance of various concepts in the development of overall theories. If this use of interpretative frameworks to explore processes such as the development of aggressive patterns of behaviour in relatively young children does occur, as it has already done in the study of adolescents, it will form a welcome extension to the research on bullying. It will also give a better basis to develop further quantitative, larger-scale studies using observational and experimental methodologies, by strengthening the theoretical framework for them. Qualitative research can do this by clarifying the psychological significance of key experiences, and by developing greater understanding of important features such as the role of the group in provoking bullying occurrences.

The different reasons for the use of quantitative or qualitative methodologies, and the research implications for the possible questions which can be asked, need far more explanation than is possible here. Investigating bullying is a very good example of a set of research questions which needs both sets of methodologies, working together.

Interpretative research in nurseries or infant schools carried out by practitioners of various kinds looking for the development of aggressive patterns of behaviour will also pose some ethical dilemmas for practitioners. How long do you let a bullying situation develop before doing something about it?

Training parents and teachers

From the earliest research efforts in evaluating the anti-bullying work going on in schools, the central and crucial role of those dealing directly with the children has been clear. Some appear to have intuitive knowledge of how to relate to the children, both those in the bullying role and those in the victim role, and are recognised as having these abilities by the children involved. When children in their schools do involve teachers in bullying situations, these are the teachers whom the children turn to, whether or not they are part of the 'official' channels of communication. However, these teachers are usually the first to be asking researchers for new ways of handling complex situations or for the latest research results. They also need colleagues who understand their activities and will play their part in implementing whole-school policies. When they move schools through promotion, their colleagues left behind are vociferous about how helpful they were to the whole anti-bullying project and how the project has suffered since they left. Their skills and knowledge, and that arising from the evaluation of anti-bullying work, has to be passed on to other teachers. In-service training may be the only possibility. The curriculum pressures of pre-service initial training from foundation subjects and the apparent centrality of children's academic attainments to current government thinking make it extremely unlikely that there will ever be any time found for effective training in anti-bullying work at the pre-service stage. Longitudinal studies of the impact of training will be necessary here.

Evaluation of induction processes for staff in schools

The problems of maintaining whole-school policies and practices over the years also point to the urgent need for effective induction training for new members of staff on anti-bullying work, and probably on a host of other pastoral care issues as well. Research into this is well overdue and would not be difficult for practitioner researchers. The methods of evaluation of in-service training are well established. The existence of reasonably well-piloted methods of establishing incidence of bullying means it may be possible to evaluate the long-term effects of training as a part of a whole-school policy, over a period of time in a particular school. General statements of the efficacy of training, however, will have to be expressed as the sum of a number of case studies into the effect of training on incidence of bullying. To enable this to happen, the reports of the evaluations of the training will need to be expressed with attention to the details of the training and its context. This topic also makes clear how deeply the application of research-based knowledge is related to evaluations of practice in each individual school. For many teacher researchers, the importance of induction training (for example) and the best general ways of carrying it out are not the issue – these questions have been thoroughly researched before. The immediate and accessible issues are: 'How effectively is my school using the knowledge available?' or 'How effective is the particular induction programme we are using?'

Evaluating parental training

One very underdeveloped anti-bullying strategy is parental training, even though we know that parents are one group that is centrally involved in supporting children and is very highly motivated to make a good job of it. Parents' role, however, is typically distrusted by children (Thompson and Arora 1991), in that the children feel their parents are likely to either over-react or under-react to the information that their child is being bullied. Parents are, however, very well aware of the need to give children a realistic and useful knowledge of how to handle aggression in social relationships, particularly parents from working-class backgrounds (Trimingham 1994). Until some researchers or practitioners specifically set up parental training programmes and evaluate them by relating these to whole-school policies and levels of bullying over a period of time, the impact of parent training can only be guessed at.

Maintaining effective anti-bullying policies and procedures

This is one of the areas where some development of theory would be very useful, as at present the findings of follow-ups of anti-bullying projects can be expressed in one common-sense word – neglect. Establishing and maintaining whole-school policies in this area require attention to a whole range of management, leadership and administrative skills, ranging from strategic management through team-building to routine administrative review. Because of the hidden nature of most bullying, it is a prime example of an activity where policy reviews need to be evidence based, from some kind of systematic data collection process. Otherwise, it is all too easy to conclude that all is (approximately) well, and no action is needed. The material of the policies, and of the reviews also, is well within the pastoral care area of responsibility, which may or may not be a significant area of knowledge of members of the senior management team. Anti-bullying policies are quite likely to be included in behaviour programmes and to run alongside other policies such as special needs policies, or anti-racist policies, with which they will partly overlap.

There are complex issues of curriculum leadership and pastoral leadership on a management level, and of recording and reviewing policies at an administrative level. To maintain curriculum interest in the anti-bullying topic over a number of years, however, the school staff need to pay attention to both curriculum planning and the teaching methods which keep the topic alive even when children have indeed 'done' it before. This continued back-up from the curriculum in the classroom in successive years to the anti-bullying work at a pastoral procedure level is one of the essential elements in maintaining the policy effectiveness (Foster and Thompson 1991). It is achieved by reframing the prosocial core of the information and discussion under other curriculum headings. The impact of the National Curriculum may have reduced the obvious scope for this type of curriculum work, but in many subject areas, particularly in the primary phase, the emphasis on skill development gives some latitude in terms of content. This aspect of anti-bullying work is hardly ever subject to evaluative research by academic researchers, but is a topic readily available for practitioner researchers.

Another aspect of efforts to maintain anti-bullying procedures is presented by the initiatives adopted by some LEA support services to establish a quality assurance procedure for the way in which schools in their authority maintain their anti-bullying policies (see Chapter 5). These aim to give schools some external reference points of procedure and a local consultancy service inside the LEA against which to assess their continuing compliance with quality standards in maintaining the policies. So far, there has been little evaluation of these developments.

Bullying after school

Almost all the work on assessing and preventing bullying has been done with reference to school-age populations. Nevertheless, we know enough about the stability of bullying behaviour and about studies of victim reports to know that it does occur in after-school years, particularly in tightly structured organisations and work-places. Intervention projects tend to be isolated. Quantitative research, other than descriptions of victims' accounts, is hard to do because of the usual reasons – the hidden nature of the bullying and access problems, the large number of other confounding variables, the difficulty of isolating the effects of any interventions if done on a small scale, and the difficulty of getting adequately large-scale interventions covering enough sites where the effects of confounding variables could be randomised. In practice, interpretative research methods would be the first choice to build up more knowledge of the processes involved. Tattum and Herbert (1997) and Randall (1996) give some examples of these intervention projects.

Conclusions

There has been much research into bullying, much has been achieved and there is much more to do. The topic penetrates into the complexities of how children develop to handle aggression appropriately and also, at the other extreme, into how schools are managed to achieve consistent, long-term policy implementation. To achieve greatest impact, researchers from different settings need to collaborate in small teams across disciplinary and institutional boundaries.

Some questions to think about

- How can school managers be encouraged to support practitioner research into anti-bullying programmes?
- How can institutions of Higher Education with research roles be encouraged to seek the views of research users in designing anti-bullying research?
- Why are longitudinal studies so rare in the anti-bullying research field? Does this matter?
- Are interviews with pupils who have bullied others sufficiently truthful to be used as research data?
- Should school managers expect to have reliable evidence on which to base policy reviews? Or should they assume 'no problem' if no more than the usual complaints are received?

Chapter 9

Conclusions: the limits of current knowledge

The principal findings from research

We have discussed many issues related to bullying, including some of the areas where the research is not complete. One theme which comes through the experience gained by teachers and researchers is how closely bullying infiltrates the day-to-day experience of school life. Much of it is invisible to the adults around because of the collusion between bullies, victims and the 'silent majority' of children who know of particular bullying relationships but do not feel individually responsible for doing anything about it. Another related theme is that, in spite of the secrecy, once the adults learn to trust the children to report accurately on their experiences in anonymous questionnaires, it is quite possible to assess the levels of bullying at particular times when the policy is being reviewed in each organisation. This enables schools to keep track of whether the levels are rising or falling in that individual organisation, one of the most useful indicators in the anti-bullying programmes. We have also seen that, given understanding and persistence, it is possible to make significant reductions in the level of bullying in schools, and that these can be maintained for a number of years if priority for this particular work is given through the school development plan or through the personal convictions of the staff involved.

Development of bullying and its relation to aggression

Aggressive behaviours between children give many causes for concern, for both parents and teachers. Not all aggression should be seen as bullying, however, as there are other reasons why pupils may be inappropriately aggressive, which teachers and other professionals become skilled at recognising. The main forms of aggressive behaviour which should not initially be seen as bullying are when it arises from emotional turbulence due to personal and social stresses, where the aggression is between two groups of children of relatively equal power or, indeed, between two individual children of relatively equal power. The UK legal definition of bullying, established by a judge in the process of hearing a case, from the variety of available definitions current at that time, is reasonably specific and could be used to advantage by the professionals:

> Bullying is long-standing violence, physical or psychological, conducted by an individual or a group and directed against an individual who is not able to defend himself in the actual situation, with a conscious desire to hurt, threaten or frighten that individual or put him under stress.
>
> (Heald 1994)

This definition, in fact, takes a number of the separate elements which had been advanced as important and blends them together. The basic process comes through clearly – a relatively long-standing dominance relationship, established and maintained by physical or psychological violence, where the victim is continually threatened and stressed at the whim of the bully.

From this definition, the question arises as to how bullying behaviour becomes established. Developmental psychologists have been researching the ways in which children learn to express aggression, how they use it to establish themselves in a group in a certain role, and how other children react to their classmates who are behaving aggressively. Social dominance, as established among children, will typically involve other kinds of behaviour: skills in talking and communicating, skills in suggesting agendas for the group to follow, even skills in anticipating the emotional reactions of the children whom the leader wishes to influence. However, one element which can be used by some children for these purposes undoubtedly is aggression. When the dominant child who uses aggression (physical or psychological) to achieve that dominance has learnt this skill, it is quite possible that achieving dominance over others through aggression will become a routine part of that child's social life. As with all learnt behaviours, there is then a debate as to whether that behaviour is most appropriately understood as a part of the child's personality or as a pattern of behaviour which can be replaced by other patterns of behaviour. One of the aspects of bullying which is very under-researched is how the behaviour of children identified during the primary-school years as being involved in bullying, either as victims or as bullies, changes as they grow older into their secondary school years. We know that the average levels of bullying reported tend to reduce slightly as children grow older, even without any intervention, but this has not yet been related to actual long-term case studies of changes in particular individuals over a number of years.

The importance of other children in the bullying pattern of behaviour

Children are clearly important as bully and victim, but there are also other children around. There are the vocal 'bully's supporters club', the group of half a dozen children who will insist, with the bully, that the whole incident was nothing like as serious as the victim portrays it – it was only a joke, at worst. There are also the 'silent majority' of children who are neither part of the bully's support group nor potential friends of the victim, who usually silently disapprove of the whole scene but who lack the confidence in themselves or trust in the adults to speak out or do anything to stop the bullying occurring. There are also the (very few) potential friends of the victim, who do what they can either to minimise the impact of the bullying or to pick up the pieces afterwards. All these are part of the group dynamics of the playground and classroom, and their presence contributes to the stability of the bullying pattern once it has emerged, and so they have to be involved in the efforts to reduce the bullying.

Another group of children who emerge in secondary schools are those who are prepared to be recruited into the school's efforts to reduce bullying – those who volunteer to be trained as counsellors in school and who join in buddy schemes, where the staff has had the time to set up such schemes. They will have varied motives for joining and will stay involved with the scheme for differing amounts of time but they, too, are a part of the group dynamics of the school.

The individuality of schools' incidence surveys

One of the slightly surprising findings to emerge from research on how much bullying occurs is that it can vary a good deal in schools of the same kind with apparently similar circumstances. One school may have two-and-a-half times the incidence of bullying, as reported by the children, as a similar school down the road, and even within schools there may be much more bullying in one particular age-cohort than another. One of the less-encouraging findings from surveys of incidence inside schools is that about 4–8 per cent of secondary school children in different schools report being bullied for more than one year; in large schools this adds up to a large number of children.

The patterns of bullying by boys and girls do seem to be different but, again, differences from school to school and from survey to survey make generalisations almost impossible. In primary schools, girls tend to bully girls and boys pick on boys, but it is likely that boy–girl bullying in secondary schools, when it occurs, will have an element of sexual harassment about it and may be seen by both the boys and the girls as a different type of interaction. Cowie (2000) gives a good summary of current research on gender issues as they interact with bullying and victimisation, and Duncan's (1999) book on sexual bullying gives a dramatic picture of the complexities of the interactions between social dominance and developing gender identities as young men and women. It also illustrates the impact which particular individual personalities have on the group dynamics of a secondary school, demonstrating the complexities which occur. Racial bullying and homophobic bullying again produce equally complex dynamics, and again generalisations of any useful kind are virtually impossible. Some of the similarities between the type of aggressive dominant behaviour in all these situations does lead to the possibility that there may be a general syndrome of 'aggressive harassment' which some children and young people develop, where they learn to apply their skills of aggressive domination to almost any situation they wish, or where the social dynamics permit them. Confirmation, however, must wait until good longitudinal research at the individual level is carried out.

The impact of bullying on the victim

A number of studies have demonstrated that being victimised is associated with truancy, various mental health problems and social isolation. Some researchers have learnt to link studies of the impact of bullying with the wider issue of stress in children. This has made them realise that the impact of the bullying is related to a number of factors, such as the level of self-esteem the child holds before the bullying, the nature of the bullying (having nasty rumours spread about oneself or one's family is consistently seen by children as the most stressful form of bullying), and length of time the bullying lasts. One study identified about one in four bullied children as showing signs of severe stress-related reactions associated with the bullying. Protective factors include supportive family relationships, good support from school personnel, and competence in other areas. Areas unresearched at present include the effects, in terms of limitations of social and academic opportunity as well as more obvious psychological damage, of mild or moderate levels of bullying on vulnerable children.

The anti-bullying project team in school

When school staff decide that the school needs an active anti-bullying policy, one of the usual courses of action is to set up a working group or committee to organise the project. To be effective, the project needs a mixture of initiatives at most of the levels in the school – the whole-school level, the class level and also the playground or lunchtime supervision level. It needs to relate to the school development plan at a very general level, to ensure recognition from senior managers that the anti-bullying project is part of the developments for the next few years. It also needs to relate to the general behaviour and discipline policies. There will be significant training needs for the teaching staff and the non-teaching support staff. If certain types of pupil-based interventions to reduce bullying, such as counselling schemes, are chosen, there will be need for pupil training as well. Part of the anti-bullying policy needs to include arrangements for reviewing the effectiveness of the project, normally on an annual basis, using accumulated evidence from surveys of various kinds. The anti-bullying project will also have an impact on the induction programme for new staff and the pastoral curriculum. The project team will need to communicate the nature of the anti-bullying project to the parents and to the new arrivals in the school each September.

The project will, in effect, be a process of general change in the school as a whole, and will need its leaders and the school managers to be aware of the nature of change processes in school. One of the school managers needs to be on the project group, to help the co-ordination of the anti-bullying project with the other aspects of school life it will influence and to act as a link with the senior management group in the school. This is also necessary to ensure the crucial continuation of the project over time – if the project becomes a series of token gestures over the succeeding three years, as 'policy drift' takes hold, then the levels of bullying are likely to increase more or less to where they were before the beginning of the programme. On the other hand, where policies are consistently implemented with clear leadership over a three- to four-year period, the bullying incidence in that school can still be going down in the fourth year after the active anti-bullying work started.

Support from the Local Education Authority

Initiatives taken by various LEAs during the 1990s have demonstrated that the anti-bullying programme is an area where education professionals based outside schools can be helpful to schools. Help ranges from training opportunities, and assessment of the incidence of bullying to the maintenance of the programmes over time. Where schools have limited expertise in the procedures necessary to set effective programmes, the external consultation and support available from LEA staff of all disciplines can be crucial to an effective programme. There are, of course, a myriad of private external consultancies happy to act as advisers in the UK, if LEA staff are thought to be too busy or too engrossed in statutory work of various descriptions.

Whole-school, group and individual interventions

As discussed above, anti-bullying interventions need to operate at a variety of levels. Some are organisational, but many need to be carried out in direct contact with the children and parents, and in ways which actively recruit those children and parents to a commitment to do what they can to help the staff reduce bullying. Most staff will need some extra training to feel confident enough to implement the anti-bullying procedures the school has chosen, as many of these procedures are different to the techniques used elsewhere in school. Some are similar to techniques which may be used already, such as active tutorial work, and staff confident in using group-work techniques will relate easily to most of them. Details of many interventions are given in Chapter 6, although many also feature in the various curriculum packs issued by local and national governments and by children's charities. Most schools should have copies of the DfEE anti-bullying pack, 'Don't suffer in silence', either in its original (1994) or updated (2000) version.

Research into bullying – achievements and priorities

Research from different types of institution has helped to clarify many of the questions about the nature of bullying and how often it occurs. It has also given some answers to questions about how effective are the various ways of intervening to reduce bullying and what school procedures are advisable to ensure the interventions continue to be effective. Research is still needed into these topics. Many of the remaining questions are essentially long-term in nature, to do with changes in children's behaviour over time, changes in patterns of organisational functioning over time, and the impact of central government policy on the effective maintenance of any school-based policies, let alone anti-bullying ones. Chapter 8 gives a detailed overview of some of these questions. These are difficult issues, requiring research methods which are well thought through and the careful incorporation of research programmes into the daily life of the school, using action research techniques as far as possible. It is possible that the current interest shown by the Teacher Training Agency in action research by teachers, through their programme of support for teacher fellowships, might make this combination of attributes for research programmes more commonly found. This will be particularly true if the members of Higher Education establish-ments can support the teacher fellows in the way the TTA is hoping for. In general, however, further progress will need careful co-operation between teachers and their school managers, local authority staff, and researchers in Higher Education institutions.

Bullying – a persistent problem

The picture we have drawn is, we believe, a hopeful one, in that it is clear that where school communities are determined to reduce bullying and are minded to approach this systematically and persis-tently, considerable change is possible. Our best estimate in this book is that, under these conditions, bullying can be reduced by about 40–50 per cent over a three- to four-year period in primary schools, and by about 20 per cent in secondary schools. Reductions such as this influence the whole climate of the school, as they demonstrate very concretely the importance of co-operation and mutual respect. These values support the anti-bullying work done by pupils, teachers and the whole school community, and influence many other school activities as well. A reduction in bullying means a reduction in chronic anxiety levels for a considerable number of children in school and increased opportunities for effective learning for all pupils.

Appendix: measuring bullying with the Life in School checklist

Background

This checklist is a collection of a number of things that might happen to a pupil in school over the duration of one week. About half of these are nice or neutral things; the other half are more unpleasant. This mixture is intended to draw attention away from the fact that the main interest is in those items that might be considered to be bullying.

The initial version of the checklist was developed by Tiny Arora in 1987, with the help of staff and pupils of Thornhill High School in Dewsbury, in order to find out whether there was bullying in the school (see Arora and Thompson 1987) and has subsequently been used in many adaptations by teachers and researchers. The present version is one that was used by the Wolverhampton Education Department for a survey of schools in their borough as part of a project on bullying (Smith 1991). Wolverhampton Education Department also developed a junior (Key Stage II) version. Both these versions are included at the end of this Appendix.

Special features

Flexibility

The checklist differs from more traditional research instruments because it exists in many different versions. The main variations are usually in the wording, in the inclusion of some of the items or in whether or not pupils are required to put their names on it. It is up to the users to decide what variations (if any) they wish to make to suit their own needs. They may, for instance, wish to know whether 'picking on someone' or 'ganging up' is happening in their school and replace some of the other items by those specific ones. Or, for age-groups below 10, they may like to make a shorter version and simplify some of the language. If this is done it is important to keep an equal proportion of positive and negative items. Also, if they wish to calculate the Bullying Index the six items mentioned on p. 186 must be kept in the checklist.

An anonymous questionnaire is likely to yield a higher response on the negative items, as many children are reluctant to admit to such actions having happened to them if they have to make themselves known.

An indirect but more precise measurement of bullying

The checklist has been designed in such a way that it is not necessary to ask the direct question: 'Are you bullied?' The main problems with asking only this direct question are:

- There are so many different types of bullying that the answer to such a question does not give any precise information about what is actually happening to the pupils.
- Many people, including children, use different definitions of bullying, so that it is difficult to know what they really mean when they confirm that they are being bullied.
- You may not wish to use the term 'bullying', as it is often an emotive one and therefore you may feel that pupils would not provide reliable responses to a direct question.
- During an intervention programme which aims to discuss bullying fully and openly, pupils become more able to detect a wider range of bullying behaviours. If, after such a programme, pupils are simply asked whether they have been 'bullied' they will use this knowledge to report a higher number of incidents as 'bullying' than they did before, thereby confounding your results.

By asking for information on specific, observable actions that could have happened to a pupil, the data will be more precise and therefore more meaningful. Such data will also give you ideas about the behaviours on which to focus an intervention programme.

The use of information from the immediate past

The pupil is asked to report only on those events that happened *during the past week*. This is important because people's recall of events that happened more than a week ago is fairly poor, and estimates based on looking further back in time are therefore more unreliable. For young pupils (below the age of 8) it will be better to ask only about what happened the day before.

What information can the checklist give?

The checklist can provide the following:

- a Bullying Index;
- a comprehensive picture of 'life in school';
- a means of identifying individuals who are likely to be victims of bullying.

Extra information of your own choice can be obtained by putting your own questions on the back page.

Indices of bullying

On the checklist designed for secondary schools, it has been found that over half of both pupils and teachers see the following items as instances of bullying:

Item 5 Tried to kick me;
Item 9 Threatened to hurt me;
Item 11 Demanded money from me;
Item 25 Tried to hurt me;
Item 38 Tried to break something of mine;
Item 40 Tried to hit me.

It has also been found that children who tick these items under the 'more than once' category are likely to see themselves as victims of bullying.

   If limited time is available for analysis and if the main interest is in bullying, then the responses to these items alone will give a quick impression of the extent of this occurring in a school. The same numbered items can be used for the Key Stage II version, but their wording is slightly different.

The main purpose of the Index is to use it like a dipstick, which can be used at the beginning of an intervention and at later intervals in order to find out whether the anti-bullying strategies are having an effect.

The Index can be used for groups of pupils of around forty or more, so it will also be possible to assess the effects which the strategies are having on different groups in the school. For groups smaller than forty, the Index will not be sufficiently reliable to allow valid comparisons.

Scoring the Bullying Index

Step 1: For each of the six items, count the number of times that a tick was placed under the category 'more than once'. Do this separately for each item (Items 5, 9, 11, 25, 38 and 40).

Step 2: Divide the scores for each separate item by the number of checklists completed. Multiply by 100 to obtain the percentage of pupil responses under each item.

Step 3: Add all the six percentages.

Step 4: Divide this number by 6. Use two decimal points – for example: 7.12 or 8.03.

The figure thus obtained is the Bullying Index.

The range of the Index can vary a great deal from school to school. Please see Table A.1 on p. 193 for the most up-to-date information.

A comprehensive picture of 'life in school'

The entire checklist can be used to obtain a more all-round picture of what happens in school during a period of one week. This is also useful for looking at a small group or for assessing how an individual pupil experiences contacts with other pupils in the school.

In the cases of groups, it will be possible to work out the percentages of the responses to each item on the checklist under the two different categories of 'once' and 'more than once'.

Identifying victims of bullying

Those pupils who tick any of the above six items under 'more than once' are likely to be most at risk of being bullied. This information can be used to identify possible victims of bullying. It has been found that two-thirds of those pupils who tick the 'more than once' column for any of the six items above will also admit that they were bullied.

The effect of asking pupils to put their names on the checklist will need to be considered, as some pupils may be more reluctant to give negative information about themselves if this is not anonymous.

Any other extra information

The back page can be used to give extra information about the bullying process. One needs to take care that there is something on this page to be completed both by children who are bullied and by those who are not, in order to avoid drawing attention to the bullied group.

How to administer

Some explanation needs to be given about why the pupils are presented with the questionnaire. This can be fairly general – for example: 'Some researchers would like to know what happens to people in school – so in this booklet are various things that might have happened to you during the past week.'

It is good practice to read out the first item for the pupils and to indicate how to complete this. Once this is done, almost all pupils find it easy to complete by themselves, except those with a reading age below 8. These pupils may require some individual assistance.

The optimum situation in which the questionnaire is completed is 'under exam conditions', as this will allow pupils most freedom to give a truthful response.

If the checklist results are to be used for comparison between groups in the school or for a yearly 'dipstick' of the whole school, then it is *very important* to keep the circumstances under which the checklist is administered as consistent as possible, as well as the instructions provided. Otherwise, variations in results are likely to be due to reasons other than the extent of bullying or aggression experienced by the pupils in your school.

Further information

It must be stressed that the main purpose of the Life in School checklist is to provide a measurement which is specific to the school and its circumstances. If such a measurement is repeated after a period of time, under the same conditions as before (i.e., same instructions, time and day of the year, and same lesson or form time), it is only then that a meaningful comparison can be made. This will, hopefully, indicate that the extent of bullying and aggression in the school is reducing and will generally help to monitor on a regular basis what is happening between pupils. However, requests are frequently received from people who have used the checklists to provide some up-to-date guidelines on how their figures compare with those of other schools. This is why those who have used the checklist have been asked to send their results to Tiny Arora, so that these can be collated in due course.

Please send any results from using the Life in School checklist to:

Dr Tiny Arora
School of Education
Sheffield University
Education Building
388 Glossop Road
Sheffield S10 2JA

Those who send in their results will receive an updated copy of Table A.1 (see p. 193).

Life in School checklist (secondary version) by Tiny Arora

I am a boy [ ]   I am a girl [ ]   Age [ ]   Year [ ]

During this week another pupil:	No	Once	More than once
1. Helped me with my homework			
2. Called me names			
3. Said something nice to me			
4. Teased me about my family			
5. Tried to kick me			
6. Was very nice to me			
7. Teased me because I am different			
8. Gave me a present			
9. Threatened to hurt me			
10. Gave me some money			
11. Demanded money from me			
12. Tried to frighten me			
13. Asked me a stupid question			
14. Lent me something			
15. Told me off			
16. Teased me			
17. Talked about clothes with me			
18. Told me a joke			
19. Told me a lie			
20. Ganged up on me			

During this week another pupil:	No	Once	More than once
21. Tried to make me hurt other people			
22. Smiled at me			
23. Tried to get me into trouble			
24. Helped me carry something			
25. Tried to hurt me			
26. Helped me with my classwork			
27. Made me do something I didn't want to			
28. Talked about T.V. with me			
29. Took something off me			
30. Shared something with me			
31. Was rude about the colour of my skin			
32. Shouted at me			
33. Played a game with me			
34. Tried to trip me up			
35. Talked about interests with me			
36. Laughed at me			
37. Threatened to tell on me			
38. Tried to break something of mine			
39. Told a lie about me			
40. Tried to hit me			

Life in School checklist (junior version) by Tiny Arora

I am a boy ☐   I am a girl ☐   Age ☐   Year ☐

During this week another pupil:	Not at all	Once	More than once
1. Called me names			
2. Said something nice to me			
3. Was nasty about my family			
4. Tried to kick me			
5. Was very nice to me			
6. Was unkind because I am different			
7. Gave me a present			
8. Said they'd beat me up			
9. Gave me some money			
10. Tried to make me give them money			
11. Tried to frighten me			
12. Asked me a stupid question			
13. Lent me something			
14. Stopped me playing a game			
15. Was unkind about something I did			
16. Talked about clothes with me			
17. Told me a joke			
18. Told me a lie			
19. Got a gang on me			
20. Tried to make me hurt other people			

During this week another pupil:	Not at all	Once	More than once
21. Smiled at me			
22. Tried to get me into trouble			
23. Helped me carry something			
24. Tried to hurt me			
25. Helped me with my classwork			
26. Made me do something I didn't want to			
27. Talked about T.V. with me			
28. Took something off me			
29. Shared something with me			
30. Was rude about the colour of my skin			
31. Shouted at me			
32. Played a game with me			
33. Tried to trip me up			
34. Talked about things I like			
35. Laughed at me horribly			
36. Said they would tell on me			
37. Tried to break something of mine			
38. Told a lie about me			
39. Tried to hit me			

Case study: Measuring bullying at Ansfield High School

This high school is situated in a large city in the Midlands area. It has about 1,200 pupils and a large staff. The intake is multi-ethnic with children from many different backgrounds, cultures and religions. Staff at the school had become concerned about instances of bullying (see also Boxes 4.1 (p. 85) and 6.2 (p. 121) in the main text). The Anti-Bullying Working Group (ABWG) decided that it needed to measure bullying for two purposes:

- to establish a baseline, so that it could see whether the incidence of bullying decreased as a result of its anti-bullying strategies;
- to gather information about where and when instances of bullying took place and ideas about what to do about bullying.

For the first purpose, a relatively easy questionnaire which was simple to administer and could be repeated on a yearly basis was selected. This was the Life in School checklist, as described earlier in this Appendix. The working group liked this particularly as it provided a Bullying Index for the whole school as well as for the different year-groups, so that it could find out and focus on any 'trouble spots'. The checklist does not actually mention the word 'bullying', which is helpful because it was felt that pupils' reports on more specific actions happening to them would give more clarity.

For the second purpose, the Anti-Bullying Working Group decided to give pupils a map of the school and asked them to shade in those areas in which they had witnessed any bullying. On the back of this map, they listed a number of questions, to be answered during a Personal, Social and Health Education period. These questions were to be discussed with the whole class group and their group response to be fed back to the ABWG.

The Bullying Index on the Life in School checklist for the whole school was 11.87. This was at the higher end of figures obtained for secondary schools (see Table A.1 in this Appendix). The map-and-questions exercise indicated that there were two areas in the school which provided particular opportunities for bullying and which needed more consistent supervision. It also indicated that there was a sizeable amount of bullying taking place in class. Pupils generated a large number of suggestions about what to do about bullying, most of these constructive and worth considering. The questions and the map exercise had been very useful and had been a starting point for discussions amongst the pupils about bullying and was felt to have had a positive effect on pupils' awareness.

- What would be the purpose of measuring bullying in your school?
- Would you wish to use the pupils' perspectives only? Who else could you survey?
- What questions would you like to ask as part of a class discussion?

Table A.1 Bullying indices on the Life in School checklist in the three phases of education in Britain (updated August 2000)

Primary phase (8–11 years)	Index	Size of school	Special details
School A	4	250–500	
School B	4.45	not known	
School C	6.42	223	Middle school; reintegrates pupils from EBD school
School D	7.6	'small'	
School E	7.87	100–250	
School F	8.98	100–250	
School G	9*	100–250	* '00 figure; in '95: 11; in '96: 9; in '97: 12; in '98: 15, in '99: 9
School H	9.4	250–500	
School I	10.83	215	Middle school
School J	11	100–250	
School K	11	100–250	Main intake from large housing estate
School L	11.26	not known	
School M	11.90	'small'	
School N	12.28	100–250	Intake from an area of social deprivation
School O	14.86	201	Middle school; includes a large 'MLD' department
School P	14.43	220	⅔ are boys; 50% ethnic minorities; middle school
School Q	15.94	100–250	
School R	18.52	135	Inner City; multi-ethnic; 50% on free school meals
Secondary phase (11–16 years)	Index	Size of school	Special details
School I	1.1*	250–500	* '99 figure; in '96: 0.93; in '97: 1.30; in '98: 0.88; Girls' res. school
School II	2	not known	Girls' school (draws on similar population as school IX)
School III	2.3	500–1000	R.C. school, drawing on inner city area
School IV	2.89	250–500	

Table A.1 (continued)

Secondary phase (11–16 years)	Index	Size of school	Special details
School V	5.71	1000+	
School VI	5.73	1000+	
School VII	6.56	500–1000	
School VIII	7.25	500–1000	
School IX	7.4	not known	Boys' school (draws on similar population as school II)
School X	7.42*	500–1000	* '99 figure. In '98: 8.83
School XI	7.78	not known	
School XII	8.59	250–500	Independent school, incl. 6th Form
School XIII	9.38	1000+	Boys' grammar school, incl. 6th Form; B.I. without 6th Form: 10.53
School XIV	10.08	500–600	
School XV	10.16	500–600	
School XVI	12.96	250–500	
School XVII	14.42	1000	Independent school; sample are all boarders – ¾ boys

Tertiary phase (16+ years)	Index	Size of school	Special details
College A	3.5	not known	

Special schools	Index	Size of school	Special details
School 1	10.00	60	EBD res.; all boys; only 45 agreed to do survey
School 2	23.39	60	EBD ⅔ are boys; 41% boarders; age range 5–12

References

Adler, P.A. and Adler, P. (1995) 'Dynamics of inclusion and exclusion in preadolescent cliques'. *Social Psychology Quarterly*, 58, 3: 145–62.

Ahmad, Y.S. (1997) *A Multimethodological Approach to Measuring Bullying in Schools*. Unpublished PhD thesis, Dept of Psychology, University of Sheffield, UK.

Archer, J. and Parker, S. (1994) 'Social representations of aggression in children'. *Aggressive Behaviour*, 20: 101–114.

Arora, C.M.J. (1994) 'Is there any point in trying to reduce bullying in secondary schools?' *Educational Psychology in Practice*, 10, 3: 155–162.

Arora, C.M.J. (1996a) *A Longitudinal Study of Secondary School Pupils' Perceptions of the Definition, Incidence and Processes of Bullying*. Unpublished PhD thesis, Sheffield University, UK.

Arora, C.M.J. (1996b) 'Defining bullying – towards a clearer understanding and more effective intervention strategies'. *School Psychology International*, 17: 317–329.

Arora, C.M.J. and Thompson, D.A. (1987) 'Defining bullying for a secondary school'. *Educational and Child Psychology*, 4 (3)(4): 110–120.

Arsenio, W.F. and Lemerise, E.A. (2001) 'Varieties of childhood bullying: values, emotional processes, and social competence'. *Social Development*, 10: 59–73.

Balding, J., Regis, D., Wise, A., Bish, D. and Muirden, J. (1996) *Bully Off: Young People that Fear Going to School*. Exeter, Schools Health Education Unit.

Balding, J., Regis, D. and Wise, A. (1998) *No Worries? Young People and Mental Health*. Exeter, Schools Health Education Unit.

Bandura, A. (1973) *Aggression: a Social Learning Analysis*. Englewood Cliffs, NJ, USA, Prentice Hall.

Bentley, K.M. and Li, A.K.F. (1995) 'Bully and victim: problems in elementary schools and students' beliefs about aggression'. *Canadian Journal of School Psychology*, 11: 153–163.

Besag, V. (1989) *Bullies and Victims in Schools*. Milton Keynes, Open University Press.

Bjørkqvist, K. and Osterman, K. (1999) 'Finland – The Nature of School Bullying', in P.K. Smith *et al.* (eds), *The Nature of School Bullying: an International Perspective*. London, Routledge.

Bjørkqvist, K., Lagerspetz, K.M.J. and Kaukiainen, A. (1992) 'Do girls manipulate and boys fight? Developmental trends regarding direct and indirect aggression'. *Aggressive Behaviour*, 18: 117–184.

Bjørkqvist, K., Ekman, K. and Lagerspetz, K. (1982) 'Bullies and victims: their ego picture, ideal ego picture and normative ego picture'. *Scandinavian Journal of Psychology*, 23: 307–313.

Bond, L., Catlin, J.B., Thomas, L., Rubin, K. and Patton, G. (2001) 'Does bullying cause emotional problems? A prospective study of young teenagers'. *British Medical Journal*, 323: 480–484.

Boulton, M. and Underwood, K. (1992) 'Bully/victim problems among middle school children'. *British Journal of Educational Psychology*, 62: 73–87.

Bowers, L., Smith, P.K. and Binney, V. (1994) 'Personal family relationships of bullies, victims, and bully/victims in middle childhood'. *Journal of Social and Personal Relationships*, 11: 215–232.

Branwhite, T. (1994) 'Bullying and student distress: the tip of the iceberg'. *Educational Psychology*, 14, 1: 59–71.

Bryant, B.K. (1992) 'Conflict resolution strategies in relation to children's peer relations'. *Journal of Applied Developmental Psychology*, 13: 35–50.

Byrne, B. (1999) 'Ireland – The Nature of School Bullying', in P.K. Smith *et al.* (eds), *The Nature of School Bullying: a Cross-National Perspective*. London, Routledge.

Campbell, A. (1996) '*Aggression, Gender and Meaning: Crossing the Sex Barrier*'. *Paper delivered at the British Psychological Society (Division of Educational and Child Psychology) Annual Course*, York University, UK.

Carr, R. (1988) 'The city-wide peer counselling program'. *Children and Youth Services Review*, 10: 217–232.

Carty, L. (1989) 'Social support, peer counselling and the community counsellor'. *Canadian Journal of Counselling*, 23: 92–102.

Childs, K. (1993) *A Follow Up Study of the Long-Term Effects of Assertiveness Training for Victims of Bullying*. Unpublished BA dissertation, Sheffield University, UK.

Chin, R. and Benne, K.D. (1976) 'General Strategies for Effecting Changes in Human Systems', in W.G. Bennis, K.D. Benne, R. Chin and K.E. Carey (eds) *The Planning of Change* (3rd edn). New York, Holt, Rinehart and Winston.

Christie, D. and Warden, D. (1997) '*Fostering Prosocial Behaviour in Schools*'. Paper presented at the British Psychological Society Education Section Annual Conference, Glasgow.

Christie, D.F.M., Warden, D.A. and Low, J.E. (1994) 'Exploring bullying and prosocial behaviour in mainstream and special schools'. *Paper presented at the BPS Education Section Annual Conference, Morecambe*, UK.

Cohen, L.H., Burt, C.E. and Bjorck, J.P. (1987) 'Life stress and adjustment: effects of life events experienced by young adolescents and their parents'. *Developmental Psychology*, 23: 4: 583–592.

Cole, R.J. (1977) *The Bullied Child in School.* Unpublished MSc dissertation, Education Dept, Sheffield University, UK.

Compas, B.E., Davis, G.E., Forsythe, C.J. and Wagner, B.M. (1987) 'Assessment of major and daily stressful events during adolescence: the adolescent perceived events scale'. *Journal of Consulting and Clinical Psychology*, 55, 4: 534–541.

Compas, B.E., Orosan, P.G. and Grant, K.E. (1993) 'Adolescent stress and coping: implications for psychopathology during adolescence'. *Journal of Adolescence*, 16: 331–349.

Conger, R.D., Xiaojia, G., Elder, G.H., Lorenz, F.O. and Simons, R.L. (1994) 'Economic stress, coercive family process and developmental problems of adolescents'. *Child Development*, 65: 541–561.

Cowie, H. (2000) 'Bystanding or standing by: gender issues in coping with bullying in English schools'. *Aggressive Behaviour* 26: 85–97.

Cowie, H., Smith, P.K., Boulton, M. and Laver, M. (1994) *Co-operation in the Multi-ethnic Classsroom: the Impact of Co-operative Group Work on Social Relationships in Middle Schools.* London, David Fulton.

Cowie, H. and Sharp, S. (1996) *Peer Counselling in Schools.* London, David Fulton.

Craig, W.M. and Pepler, D.J. (1992) *Contextual Factors in Bullying and Victimization.* Paper presented at the Canadian Psychological Association Conference, Toronto.

Crick, N. and Grotpeter, J. (1995) 'Relational aggression, gender and socio-psychological adjustment'. *Child Development*, 66: 710–722.

Dale, R.R. (1991) 'Mixed Versus Single Sex Schools: the Social Aspect of Bullying', in M. Elliott (ed), *Bullying: a Practical Guide to Coping for Schools.* Harlow, UK, Longman.

Dawkins, R. (1976) *The Selfish Gene.* Oxford, Oxford University Press.

DeCecco, J. and Richards, A. (1974) *Growing Pains: Uses of School Conflict.* New York, Aberdeen Press.

Department for Education and Employment (1994) 'Don't Suffer in Silence'. DfEE, London.

Department for Education and Employment (2000) 'Don't Suffer in Silence'. (2nd edn). DfEE, London.

De Rosenroll, D.A. (1989) 'A practitioner's guide to peer counselling: research issues and dilemmas'. *Canadian Journal of Counselling*, 23: 75–91.

DeRosier, M.E., Cillessen, A.H.N., Coie, J.D. and Dodge, K.A. (1994) 'Group social context and children's aggressive behaviour'. *Child Development*, 65: 1068–1079.

Dodge, K.A. (1991) 'The Structure and Function of Reactive and Proactive Aggression', in D. Pepler and K. Rubin (eds), *The Development and Treatment of Childhood Aggression*. NJ, USA, Lawrence Erlbaum Associates.

Dollard, J., Doob, L. W., Miller, N. E., Mowrer, O. H. and Sears, D. R. (1939) *Frustration and Aggression*. New Haven, Conn., USA, Yale University Press.

DuBois, D.L., Felner, R.D., Brand, S., Adan, A.M. and Evans, E.G. (1992) 'A prospective study of life stress, social support and adaptation in early adolescence'. *Child Development*, 63: 542–557.

Duncan, N. (1999) *Sexual Bullying: Gender Conflict and Pupil Culture in Secondary Schools*. London, Routledge.

Elias, M.J. and Clabby, J.F. (1992) *Building Social Problem Solving Skills: Guidelines from a School Based Programme*. New York, Institute for Rational Living.

Emery, R.E. and Forehand, R. (1994) 'Parental Divorce and Children's Wellbeing: a Focus on Resilience', in R.J. Haggerty, L.R. Sherrod, N. Garmezy and M. Rutter (eds), *Stress, Risk and Resilience in Children and Adolescents: Processes, Mechanisms and Interventions*. Cambridge, Cambridge University Press.

Eron, L.D. Huesmann, R.L., Dubow, E., Romanoff, R. and Yarmel, P.W. (1987) 'Aggression and its Correlates Over 22 Years', in D. Growell, I. Evans and C. O'Donnell (eds), *Childhood Aggression and Violence*. New York, Plenum Press.

Eslea, M. (1997) *Pupils, Parents and Teachers: Building a United Opposition to Bullying*. Unpublished PhD Thesis, Dept of Psychology, Sheffield University.

Eslea, M., and Smith, P.K. (1994) *Developmental Trends in Attitudes to Bullying*. Poster presentation at the Thirteenth Bienniel Meeting of ISSBD, Amsterdam.

Eslea, M. and Smith, P.K. (1998) 'The long-term effectiveness of anti-bullying work in primary schools'. *Educational Research*, 40: 203–218.

Eslea, M. and Smith, P.K. (2000) 'Pupil and parent attitudes toward bullying in primary schools'. *European Journal of Psychology of Education*, 15: 207–219.

Everhart, R.B. (1983) *Reading, Writing and Resistance. Adolescence and Labour in a Junior High School*. London, Routledge and Kegan Paul.

Fabre-Cornelli, D., Emin, J.C. and Pain, J. (1999) 'France', in P.K. Smith *et al.* (eds), *The Nature of School Bullying: a Cross-National Perspective*. London, Routledge.

Farrington, D.P. (1991) 'Childhood Aggression and Adult Violence: Early Precursors and Later-life Outcomes', in D. Pepler and K. Rubin (eds), *The Development and Treatment of Childhood Aggression*. Hillsdale, NJ, Lawrence Erlbaum.

Felner, R.D., Brand, S., DuBois, D.L., Adan, A.M., Mulhall, P.F. and Evans, E.G. (1995) 'Socio-economic disadvantage, proximal environmental experiences and socio-emotional and academic adjustment in early adolescence: investigation of a mediated effects model'. *Child Development*, 66: 774–792.

Fonzi, A., Genta, M. L., Menesini, E., Bacchini, D., Bonino, S. and Costabile, A. (1999) 'Italy – The Nature of School Bullying', in P.K. Smith *et al.* (eds), *The Nature of School Bullying: a Cross-National Perspective*. London, Routledge.

Foster, P. and Thompson, D.A. (1991) 'Bullying – Towards a Non-violent Sanctions Policy', in P.K. Smith and D.A. Thompson (eds), *Practical Approaches to Bullying*. London, David Fulton.

Freud, S. (1920) 'A general introduction to psycho-analysis'. *Elementary School Journal* 88: 79–92.

Gardner, H. (1993) *The Unschooled Mind*. London, Fontana.

Garmezy, N. and Rutter, M. (eds) (1983) *Stress, Coping and Development in Children*. New York, McGraw-Hill.

Garmezy, N. and Masten, A. (1991) 'The Protective Role of Competence Indicators in Children at Risk', in E.M. Cummings, A.L. Greene and K.H. Karraker (eds), *Life Span Developmental Psychology: Perspectives on Stress and Coping*. Hillsdale, NJ, Lawrence Erlbaum.

Garton, A.F. and Pratt, C. (1995) 'Stress and self concept in 10 to 15 year olds'. *Journal of Adolescence*, 18: 625–640.

Genta, M.L., Menesini, E., Fonzi, A. and Costabile, A. (1996) 'Bullies and victims in schools in central and southern Italy'. *European Journal of Psychology of Education*, 11 (1): 97–110.

Gibson-Cline, J. (1996) *Adolescence – From Crisis to Coping: a Thirteen Nation Study*. Oxford, Butterworth-Heinemann Ltd.

Gillborn, D. (1990) *Teaching and Learning in Multi-ethnic Schools*. London, Unwin-Hyman.

Goleman, D. (1996) *Emotional Intelligence*. London, Bloomsbury.

Gore, S. and Colten, M. (1991) 'Gender, Stress and Distress: Social-relational Influences', in J. Eckenrode (ed), *The Social Context of Coping*. New York, Plenum Press.

Greenberg, M.T., Kusche, C.A., Cooke, E.T. and Quamma, J.P. (1950) 'Promoting emotional competence in school aged children: the effects of the paths curriculum'. *Development and Psychopathology*, 7: 7–16.

Haapasalo, J. and Tremblay, R. E. (1994) 'Physically aggressive boys from age 6 to 12: family background, parenting behaviour and prediction of delinquency'. *Development and Psychopathology*, 8: 443–455.

Hartup, W. (1974) 'Aggression in childhood: developmental perspectives'. *American Psychologist*, 29: 336–341.

Haselager, G.J.T. and Van Lieshout, C.F.M. (1992) *Social and Affective Adjustment of Self and Peer Reported Victims and Bullies*. Paper presented at the 5th European Conference on Developmental Psychology, Seville.

Hatch, A.J. (1987) 'Status and social power in a kindergarten peer group'. *Elementary School Journal*, 88(1): 79–92.

Hawker, D.S.J. and Boulton, M.J. (2000) 'Twenty years of research on peer victimisation and psychosocial maladjustment: a meta-analytic review of cross-sectional studies'. *Journal of Child Psychology and Psychiatry*, 41: 441–455.

Hazzan, K. (1991) *Is Bullying Upsetting? An Investigation of Stresses in Infant School Children*. Unpublished MSc Thesis, Department of Education, Sheffield University.

Heald, T.R. (1994) *Judgement in the case between R.H. Walker and Derbyshire County Council*. Nottingham, County Court Records.

Heinemann, P. P. (1973) *Mobbning. Gruppvald Blant Barn og. Vokane*. Stockholm, Natur och Kultur.

Hendren, R.L. (1990) 'Stress in Adolescence', in L. Eugene Arnold (ed), *Childhood Stress*. New York, John Wiley.

Henry, J.P. (1980) 'Present Concepts of Stress Theory', in E. Ursdin, R. Kvetnansky and I.J. Copin (eds), *Catecholamines and Stress*. New York, Elsevier.

Holmes, T.H. and Rahe, R.H. (1967) 'The social readjustment rating scale'. *Journal of Psychosomatic Research*, 11: 213–218.

Hoover, J.H., Oliver, R. and Hazler, R.J. (1992) 'Bullying: perceptions of adolescent victims in the Midwestern USA'. *School Psychology International*, 13: 5–16.

Humphries, A. and Smith, P.K. (1987) 'Rough and tumble, friendship and dominance in schoolchildren: evidence for continuity and change with age'. *Child Development*, 58: 201–212.

Hyde, J. (1986) 'Gender Differences in Aggression', in J.Hyde and M.Linn (eds), *The Psychology of Gender: Advances Through Meta-Analysis*. Baltimore, USA, Johns Hopkins University Press.

Jacobs, R.W. (1994) *Real Time Strategic Change*. San Francisco, Berrett-Koehler.

Johnson, D.W. and Johnson, R.T. (1989) *Cooperation and Competition*. Minnesota, Interaction Book Co.

Jones, E.E. and Pittman, T.S. (1982) 'Toward a general theory of strategic self-presentation', in J.Suls (ed) *Psychological Perspectives on the Self*. Hillsdale, NJ, Lawrence Erlbaum.

Kalliotis, P.A. (1994) *A Comparison of the Incidence of Bullying in English and Greek Schools for 11-year-old Pupils*. Unpublished MEd Dissertation, Education Department, University of Sheffield.

Kimchi, J. and Schaffner, B. (1990) 'Childhood Protective Factors and Stress Risk', in L. Eugene Arnold (ed), *Childhood Stress*. New York, John Wiley.

Kingston Friends Workshop Group (1987) *Ways and Means: An Approach to Problem Solving*. London, Kingston Friends Workshop Group.

Kreidler, W.J. (1984) *Creative Conflict Resolution*. Glenview, Illinois, Scott Foresman and Co.

La Fontaine, J. (1991) *Bullying: the Child's View*. London, Calouste Gulbenkian Foundation.

Lagerspetz, K., Bjørkqvist, K. and Peltonen, T. (1988) 'Is indirect aggression typical of females? Gender differences in aggressiveness in 11–12 year old children'. *Aggressive Behaviour*, 14: 403–414.

Latané, B. and Darley, J.M. (1970) *The Unresponsive Bystander – why Doesn't he Help?* Englewood Cliffs, NJ, Prentice Hall.

Latané, B. and Nida, S. (1981) 'Ten years of research on group size and helping'. *Psychological Bulletin* 89(2): 308–324.

Lazarus, R.S. and Folkman, S. (1984) *Stress, Appraisal and Coping*. New York, Springer.

Lewin, K. (1947) 'Group Decisions and Social Change', in T. Newcomb and E. Hartley (eds), *Readings in Social Psychology*. New York, Holt, Rinehart and Winston.

Loeber, R. and Stouthamer-Loeber, M. (1998) 'Juvenile Aggression at Home and at School', in D. Elliott, B. Hamburg and K. Williams (eds) *Violence in American Schools*. Cambridge, Cambridge University Press.

Lowenstein, L. F. (1978) 'Who is the bully?' *Bulletin of the British Psychological Society*, 31: 147–149.

Mac An Ghaill, M. (1995) '(In)visibility – Race, Sexuality and Masculinity in the School Context', in M.Blair, J.Holland and S. Sheldon (eds), *Identity and Diversity – Gender and the Experience of Education*. Milton Keynes, Open University Press.

MacLeod, M. and Morris, S. (1996) *Why Me? Children talking to Childline about Bullying*. London, Childline.

McCaffrey, T. and Lyons, E. (1993) 'Teaching children to be good friends – developmental groupwork with vulnerable children'. *Educational and Child Psychology*, 10: 3.

Madsen, K. (1997) *Differing Perceptions of Bullying*. Unpublished PhD Thesis, Department of Psychology, Sheffield University.

Maines, B. and Robinson, G. (1992) *The No Blame Approach*. Bristol, Lucky Duck Publishing.

Mellor, A. (1990) *Bullying in Scottish secondary schools*. Edinburgh, Scottish Council for Research in Education.

Mellor Smith, H. (1992) *The Effect of Quality Circles on Bullying Behaviour in Schools*. Unpublished BA dissertation. Sheffield University.

Menesini, E., Eslea, M., Smith, P.K., Genta, M.L., Giannetti, E., Fonzi, A. and Costabile, A. (1996) 'A cross-national comparison of children's attitudes towards bully/victim problems in school'. *Aggressive Behaviour*, 23 (4): 245–257.

Mykletun, R. J. (1979) *Plagen i Skolen*. Stavanger, Rogalands forskning.

Nabuzoka, D. (1999) 'A comparison of the experiences of bullying behaviour by English and Zambian pupils.' Unpublished paper, Department of Education, Sheffield Hallam University.

Naylor, P. and Cowie, H. (1999) 'The effectiveness of peer support systems in challenging school bullying: perceptions of teachers and pupils'. *Journal of Adolescence*, 22, 34: 467–479.

Neary, A. and Joseph, S. (1994) 'Peer victimisation and its relationship to self concept and depression among schoolgirls'. *Personality and Individual Differences*, 16, 1: 183–186.

O'Connor, C.A. (1993) 'Organisational behaviour: where we've been, where we're going'. *Annual Review of Psychology*, 42: 427–458.

Olweus, D. (1978) *Aggression in the Schools: Bullies and Whipping-boys*. London, Wiley; Halsted Press.

Olweus, D. (1980) 'Familial and temperamental determinants of aggressive behaviour in adolescent boys'. *Developmental Psychology*, 16: 644–660.

Olweus, D. (1991) 'Bully/victim Problems amongst School Children: Basic Facts and Effects of a School Based Intervention Program', in D. Pepler and K. Rubin (eds), *The Development and Treatment of Childhood Aggression*. Hillsdale, NJ, Lawrence Erlbaum.

Olweus, D. (1993) *Bullying at School: What we Know and What We Can Do*. Oxford, Blackwell.

Olweus, D. (1999) 'Norway', in P.K. Smith *et al.* (eds), *The Nature of School Bullying – a Cross-National Perspective*. London, Routledge.

Pearlin, L.I. (1991) 'The Study of Coping: an Overview of Problems and Directions', in J. Eckenrode (ed), *The Social Context of Coping*. New York, Plenum Press.

Pellegrini, A.D. and Bartini, M. (2001) 'Dominance in early adolescent boys: affiliative and aggressive dimensions and possible functions'. *Merrill-Palmer Quarterly*, 47: 142–163.

Pepler, D.J., Craig, W., Zeigler, S. and Charach, A. (1993) 'A School-based Anti-bullying Intervention: Preliminary Evaluation', in D. Tattum (ed), *Understanding and Managing Bullying*. Oxford, Heinemann.

Pepler, D.J. and Craig, W.M. (1995) 'A peek behind the fence: naturalistic observations of aggressive children with remote audiovisual recording'. *Developmental Psychology*, 31: 548–553.

Pervin, K. and Turner, A. (1994) 'An investigation into staff and pupils' knowledge, attitudes and beliefs about bullying in an inner city school'. *Pastoral Care in Education*, 12, 3: 16–21.

Pikas, A. (1989) 'The Common Concern Method for the Treatment of Mobbing', in E. Roland and E. Munthe (eds), *Bullying: An International Perspective*. London, David Fulton.

Priest, S. (2001) 'Quality assurance for anti-bullying policies in schools'.

Unpublished paper, Research Dissemination Seminar 'Effective Maintenance of Anti-Bullying Policies', School of Education, Sheffield University, March 2001.

Pryor-Brown, L., Cowen, E.L., Hightower, A.D. and Lofyczewski, B.S. (1986) 'Demographic differences among children in judging and experiencing specific stressful life events'. *The Journal of Special Education*, 20: 339–345.

Randall, P. (1996) *A Community Approach to Bullying*. Trentham, UK, Trentham Books.

Reid, K. (1989) 'Bullying and Persistent School Absenteeism', in D. Tattum and D. Lane (eds), *Bullying in Schools*. Stoke on Trent, Trentham Books.

Rice, K.G., Herman, M.A. and Peterson, A.C. (1993) 'Coping with challenge in adolescence: a conceptual model and psycho-educational intervention'. *Journal of Adolescence*, 16: 235–251.

Rigby, K. (1996) *Bullying in School, and What to Do About it*. London, Jessica Kingsley Publishers.

Rigby, K. (1999) 'Peer victimisation at school and health of secondary school students'. *British Journal of Educational Psychology*. 69: 95–104.

Rigby, K. and Slee, P. (1991) 'Bullying among Australian school children: reported behaviour and attitudes towards victims'. *Journal of Social Psychology*, 31: 615–627.

Rigby, K. and Slee, P. (1993a) 'Children's Attitudes Towards Victims', in D.Tattum (ed), *Understanding and Managing Bullying*. London, Heinemann Educational.

Rigby, K. and Slee, P. (1993b) 'Dimensions of interpersonal relating among Australian school children and their implications for psychological wellbeing'. *Journal of Social Psychology*, 133, 1: 33–42.

Rivers, I. (1995) 'The victimisation of gay teenagers in school: homophobia in education'. *Pastoral Care in Education*, 13: 35–41.

Rivers, I. (1996) 'Protecting the gay adolescent at school'. *Medicine, Mind and Adolescence*, 11, 2: 15–24.

Rivers, I. (2000a) 'Social exclusion, absenteeism and sexual minority youth'. *Support for Learning*, 15, 1: 13–18.

Rivers, I. (2000b) 'Retrospective reports of bullying at school'. *British Journal of Development Psychology*, 18: 20–27.

Rogers, E. and Shoemaker, F. (1971) *Communication and Innovation*. New York, Free Press.

Roland, E. (1989a) 'Bullying. The Scandinavian Research Tradition', in D. P. Tattum and D. A. Lane (eds), *Bullying in Schools*. Stoke-on-Trent, Trentham Books.

Roland, E. (1989b) 'A System-Orientated Strategy against Bullying', in E. Roland and E. Munthe (eds), *Bullying: an International Perspective*. London: David Fulton.

Roland, E. (1993) 'Bullying: developing a tradition of research and management', in D.P.Tattum (ed), *Understanding and Managing Bullying*. Oxford, Heinemann Educational.

Roland, E. (1998) *School Influences on Bullying*. Unpublished PhD Thesis, Department of Education, University of Durham.

Roland, E. and Munthe, E. (eds) (1989) *Bullying: an International Perspective*. London, David Fulton.

Roland, E. and Munthe, E. (1997) 'The 1996 Norwegian Programme for preventing and managing bullying in schools'. *Irish Journal of Psychology*, 18, 2: 233–247.

Rutter, M. (1994) 'Stress Research: Accomplishments and Tasks Ahead', in R.J. Haggerty, L.R. Sherrod, N. Garmezy and M. Rutter (eds), *Stress, Risk and Resilience in Children and Adolescents: Processes, Mechanisms and Interventions*. Cambridge, Cambridge University Press.

Ryan, N.M. (1989) 'Identification of children's coping strategies from the school-agers perspective'. *Research in Nursing and Health*, 12: 111–122.

Ryan-Wenger, N.M. (1990) 'Children's psychosomatic responses to stress', in L. Eugene Arnold (ed), *Childhood Stress*. New York, John Wiley.

Salmivalli, C. (1998) *Not Only Bullies and Victims: Participation in Harassment in School Classes – some Social and Personality Factors*. Doctoral Dissertation, University of Turku, Finland.

Salmivalli, C., Huttunen, A. and Lagerspetz, K. (1997) 'Peer networks and bullying in schools'. *Scandinavian Journal of Psychology*, 38(4): 305–312.

Salmivalli, C., Karhunen, J. and Lagerspetz, K. (1996a) 'How do the victims respond to bullying?' *Aggressive Behaviour*, 22: 99–109.

Salmivalli, C., Lagerspetz, K., Bjørkvist, K. and Østerman, K. (1996b) 'Bullying as a group process: participant roles and their relations to social status within the group'. *Aggressive Behaviour*, 22(1): 1–15.

Savin-Williams, R. C. (1976) 'Social Interactions of Adolescent Females in Natural Groups', in H. Foot, H.J. Chapman and J.R. Smith (eds), *Friendship and Social Relations in Children*. Chichester, John Wiley.

Savin-Williams, R. C. (1977) 'Dominance in a human adolescent group'. *Animal Behaviour*, 25: 400–406.

Savin-Williams, R. C. (1980) 'Dominance and Submission among Early Adolescent Boys', in D.R. Omark, F.F.Strayer and D.G.Freedman (eds), *Dominance Relations. An Ethological View of Human Conflict and Social Interaction*. New York, London, Garland STPM Press.

Sears, S.J. and Milburn, J. (1990) 'School Age Stress', in L. Eugene Arnold (ed), *Childhood Stress*. New York, John Wiley and Sons.

Sharp, S. (1995) *Self-esteem, Response Style, and Victimisation: Possible Ways of Preventing Victimisation through Parenting and School Based Training Programmes*. Paper presented at the European Conference on Educational Research (B.E.R.A), University of Bath.

Sharp, S. (1995) 'How much does bullying hurt? The effects of bullying on the health, happiness and educational progress of secondary aged students'. *Educational and Child Psychology*.

Sharp, S. (1997) *Bullying in Schools – a Study of Stress and Coping amongst Secondary aged Students who have been Bullied*. Unpublished PhD Thesis, Department of Education, Sheffield University.

Sharp, S. and Cowie, H. (1994) 'Empowering students to take Positive Action Against Bullying', in P.K. Smith and S. Sharp (eds), *School Bullying: Insights and Perspectives*. London, Routledge.

Sharp, S. and Thompson, D. (1994) 'The Role of Whole School Policies in Tackling Bullying in Schools'. In P.K. Smith and S. Sharp (eds), *School Bullying: Insights and Perspectives*. London, Routledge.

Sharp, S. and Smith, P.K. (eds) (1994) *How to Tackle Bullying in Your School: a Practical Handbook for Teachers*. London: Routledge.

Silverman, W.K., LaGreca, A.M. and Wasserstein, S. (1995) 'What do children worry about? Worries and their relation to anxiety'. *Child Development*, 66: 671–686.

Skinner, A. (1992) *Bullying: an Annotated Bibliography of Literature and Resources*. Leicester, Youth Work Press.

Smith, G. (1991) *The Safer Cities, Safer Schools Project*. Wolverhampton, Wolverhampton Education Department.

Smith, P.K. and Thompson, D.A (eds) (1991) *Practical Approaches to Bullying*. London, David Fulton.

Smith, P.K. and Sharp, S. (eds) (1994) *School Bullying: Insights and Perspectives*. London, Routledge.

Smith, P.K. and Levan, S. (1995) 'Perceptions and Experiences of Bullying in Younger Pupils'. *British Journal of Educational Psychology*, 65: 485–500.

Smith, P.K., Madsen, K. and Moody, J. (1999) 'What causes the age decline in reports of being bullied at school? Towards a developmental analysis of the risks of being bullied'. *Educational Research* 41: 267–285.

Stanley, L. and Arora, C.M.J. (1998) 'Social exclusion amongst adolescent girls – their self-esteem and coping strategies'. *Educational Psychology in Practice* 14, 2: 22–28.

Staub, E. (1970) 'A child in distress: the influence of age and number of witnesses on children's attempts to help'. *Journal of Personality and Social Psychology*, 14: 130–140.

Stephenson, P. and Smith, D. (1987) 'Anatomy of a playground bully'. *Education*. Stoke on Trent, Trentham Books.

Stephenson, P. and Smith, D. (1989) 'Bullying in the Junior School', in D.P. Tattum and D.A. Lane (eds), *Bullying in Schools*. Trentham.

Stephenson, P. and Smith, D. (1991) 'Why some schools don't have bullies', in M. Elliott (ed), *Bullying: a Practical Guide to Coping for Schools*. Harlow, Longman.

Sullivan, K. (2000) *The Anti-Bullying Handbook*. Oxford, Oxford University Press.

Sutton, J. (2001) 'Bullies: thugs or thinkers?' *The Psychologist*, 14, 10: 530–534.

Sutton, J. and Keogh, E. (2000) 'Social competition in school: relationships with bullying, Machiavellianism and personality'. *British Journal of Educational Psychology*, 70: 443–457.

Swick, K. and Hassell, T. (1990) 'Parental efficacy and the development of social competency in young children'. *Journal of Instructional Psychology*, 17: 24–32.

Tattum, D.P. (ed) (1993) *Understanding and Managing Bullying*. Oxford, Heinemann.

Tattum, D.P. and Lane, D.A. (eds) (1989) *Bullying in Schools*. Stoke on Trent, Trentham Books.

Tattum, D.P. and Herbert, G. (1997) *Bullying: Home, School, and Community*. London, David Fulton.

Taylor, G. (1996) 'Creating a Circle of Friends: a Case Study', in H. Cowie and S. Sharp (eds), *Peer Counselling in Schools: a Time to Listen*. London, David Fulton.

Tedeschi, J. T. (1984) 'A Social Psychological Interpretation of Human Aggression', in A. Mummendey (ed), *Social Psychology of Aggression*. Berlin, Heidelberg, Springer-Verlag.

Tedeschi, J.T. and Felson, R.B. (1994) *Violence, Aggression and Coercive Actions*. Washington, DC, APA Press.

Thompson, D.A. (1995) *Two Years On: Problems in Monitoring Anti-bullying Policies in School and Their Effect on the Incidence of Bullying*. Paper presented at the BERA/EERA European Conference of Educational Research, University of Bath.

Thompson, D.A. and Arora, C.M.J. (1991) 'Why do children bully? An evaluation of the long-term effectiveness of a whole-school policy to minimize bullying'. *Pastoral Care in Education*, December 1991: 8–12.

Thompson, D.A. and Sharp, S. (1994) *Improving Schools: Establishing and Integrating Whole School Behaviour Policies*. London, David Fulton.

Tonge, D. (1992) *Assessing the Effects of Assertiveness Training on Victims of Bullying in Three Sheffield Schools*. Unpublished BA dissertation, University of Sheffield.

Torgerson, A.M. (1995) 'Temperament Research in Scandinavia', in G.A. Kohnstamm, J.E. Bates and M.K. Rothbart (eds), *Temperament in Childhood*. Chichester, John Wiley.

Trad, P.V. and Greenblatt, E. (1990) 'Psychological Aspects of Child Stress: Development and the Spectrum of Coping Responses', in L. Eugene Arnold (ed), *Childhood Stress*. New York, John Wiley.

Trimingham, C. (1994) *Bullying Involving Statemented Children in Main-stream Schools*. Unpublished MSc Thesis, Department of Education, University of Sheffield.

Turner, A.K. (1994) 'Genetic and Hormonal Influences on Male Violence', in J. Archer (ed), *Male Violence*. London, Routledge.

Wachtel, P.L. (1973) 'Psychodynamics, behaviour therapy and the implacable experimenter: an inquiry into the consistency of personality'. *Journal of Abnormal Psychology*, 83: 324–334.

Warden, D.A. and Christie, D.F.M. (1997) *Teaching Social Behaviour: Classroom Activities to Foster Children's Interpersonal Awareness.* London, David Fulton.

Werner, E.E. (1989) 'High risk children in young adulthood: a longitudinal study from birth to age 32'. *American Journal of Orthopsychiatry*, 59 (1): 72–78.

Whitney, I. and Smith, P.K. (1993) 'A survey of the nature and extent of bullying in junior/middle and secondary schools'. *Educational Research* 35, 1: 3–25.

Whitney, I., Smith, P.K. and Thompson, D.A. (1994) 'Bullying and Children with Special Educational Needs', in Smith, P.K. and Sharp, S. (eds), *School Bullying: Insights and Perspectives*. London, Routledge.

Wood, D., Wood, H., Griffiths, A.J. and Howarth, I. (1986) *Teaching and Talking with Deaf Children*. London, Wiley.

Yamamoto, K., Suliman, A., Parsons, J. and Davies Jr., O.L. (1987) 'Voices in unison: stressful events in the lives of children in six countries'. *Journal of Child Psychology and Psychiatry*, 28, 6: 855–864.

Ziegler, S. and Rosenstein-Manner, M. (1991) *Bullying in School*. Toronto, Board of Education.

Index